Prentice Hall's e-marketing Guide

PRENTICE HALL
E-Business

2001 edition

RAYMOND D.   JUDY
FROST   STRAUSS

Ohio University   *University of Nevada - Reno*

Prentice
Hall

Prentice Hall Upper Saddle River, NJ 07458

Cover design: *Michael Fruhbeis*
Acquisitions editor: *Whitney Blake*
Associate editor: *Anthony Palmiotto*
Project editor: *Theresa Festa*
Manufacturer: *Victor Graphics, Inc.*

© 2001 by Prentice Hall, Inc.
Upper Saddle River, New Jersey 07458

All rights reserved. No part of this book may be reproduced, in any form or by any means, electronic or mechanical, including photocopying, recording, or any information storage and retrieval system, without permission in writing from the Publisher.

Printed in the United States of America

10   9   8   7   6   5   4   3   2

ISBN 0-13-030656-8

TRADEMARK INFORMATION
Adapted from Ping, Alstair: Social Conscience for Sales, Marketing, Sept 1993, pp. 22, American Marketing Association, with permission.

Reproduced with permission of Yahoo! Inc. Copyright © 2000 by YAHOO! And the YAHOO! logo are trademarks of Yahoo! Inc.

These materials have been reproduced by Prentice Hall with the permission of eBay Inc. Copyright© eBay Inc. All rights reserved.

Amazon.com is a registered trademark or trademark of Amazon.com, Inc. in the U.S. and/or other countries. © 2000 by Amazon.com. All rights reserved.

© 2000 The New York Times Company. Reprinted by Permission.

Prentice-Hall International (UK) Limited, *London*
Prentice-Hall of Australia Pty. Limited, *Sydney*
Prentice-Hall Canada Inc., *Toronto*
Prentice-Hall Hispanoamericana, S.A., *Mexico*
Prentice-Hall of India Private Limited, *New Delhi*
Prentice-Hall of Japan, Inc., *Tokyo*
Prentice-Hall (Singapore) Pte Ltd
Editora Prentice-Hall do Brasil, Ltda., *Rio de Janeiro*

Contents

Preface

The Internet's rapid growth is reminiscent of television's early years. Something important and historic is happening; we are in the middle of a story with an unpredictable outcome. Users world-wide are adopting the Net at an incredible rate, companies are jumping on the bandwagon to display their wares, but technology and other factors currently limit the Internet from reaching its full potential. Will the future Internet provide complete digital multimedia programming on demand, thus making traditional media distribution channels obsolete? Will online shopping and advertising revenues grow to larger proportions than their traditional counterparts? We've seen the Internet become mainstream, at least in the U.S., since we wrote the first edition of this guide in fall 1996. How will the Net look in another five years? One thing is certain: it is exciting to hypothesize about the Net's future!

We believe that the Internet is emerging both as an extremely useful tool for business planning and also as part of a company's marketing mix. As tools, the Internet search and resource sites can aid any discipline by opening a high-speed gateway to a wealth of information. Also, the Net facilitates text-based communication via e-mail newsgroups and mailing lists. In the marketing discipline, the Internet serves as distribution channel, communication medium, and fertile ground for new products. Marketers use the Net for direct distribution of digital products, for electronic storefronts, and for distribution channel member collaboration. The Net marketing communication function includes advertising, public relations, direct marketing, and sales promotion. Finally, Internet technologies created the opportunity for a variety of innovative services including shopping agents, stock trading, and online auctions. What's next?

The fifth edition of *The Internet: A New Marketing Tool* rests on this vision of the Net. In fact, the Net is now so firmly entrenched in marketing practice that we've changed the book name to *Prentice Hall's e-Marketing Guide, 2001*. Improvements in the fifth edition include:

- Up to date Internet terminology and business models
- New and updated Leveraging Technology sections to help marketers understand the important technologies that facilitate marketing goals
- Improved screen shots and explanatory diagrams
- Less emphasis on concepts already familiar to students

Workbook Pedagogy

1. **Principles of marketing.** This workbook is designed to accompany a principles of marketing text. Both its content and organization reflect this design. Each chapter can be assigned as a stand-alone exercise, not requiring information from previous chapters. We recommend that students complete the search exercises in Chapter 1, however, so that their work in subsequent chapters will be more efficient. Although most students know how to use search tools, these exercises introduce advanced concepts.

2. **Chapter structure.** Each chapter begins with an outline and learning objectives. Next is a thorough description of the topic and how it relates to marketing on the Internet. This is followed by an exercise. Each exercise provides a short explanation of various Web sites, and presents a series of questions interspersed with more explanations. The exercise often concludes with a "putting it together"

exercise as a summary of chapter findings. The chapter concludes with a "leveraging technology" section that explains how technological innovations are turned into business opportunities. We also indicate the estimated length of time it should take to read the chapter and complete the exercise.

3. **Active learning.** When students actively participate in the learning process, learning is enhanced. Through the hands-on approach in this workbook, students discover solutions to real marketing problems and in the process gain insight and experience with Internet navigation and content.

4. **Guided exploration.** Students are directed to particular Web sites and asked to answer questions. In this way active learning is directed learning. For example, we describe the Net's role for market analysis using secondary data and then send students to various sites to conduct an environmental scan for a new car introduction. To answer the questions, students must find information at the sites and offer opinions about findings.

5. **Application and analysis.** In many exercises, students must analyze the information from Web sites to answer marketing questions. One chapter focuses on Net users, directing students to sites reporting on demographics, geographics, psychographics and Net behavior. We ask students to describe the profile of a typical Net user and then to design an online magazine that would appeal to that user.

6. **Net experience.** We assume that users of this workbook know how to log on and use a graphical Web browser. There are many other helpful books if this is not the case with your students. We have tried to make our instructions generic enough so that any browser may be used.

We strongly recommend that you remain flexible while using this workbook. By the time you introduce it, many sites may have changed (see the section, "Why there are mistakes in this book"). Nevertheless, our experience is that inventive students will find alternative solutions to most exercise problems. For example, in one class students were exploring the Net as an online storefront, and the site they were trying to access was down. While waiting, one student asked to order pizza over the Net. The class spent the next 15 minutes trying to find an electronic storefront to order food for the class. This exercise familiarized students with the use of search engines. It is this sort of discovery learning which sparks excitement and provides value to instructors and students. After all, we are all students of marketing, and nowhere is this so evident as with the Internet.

Instructor's Resources

The Internet is loaded with free resources to aid in teaching at the University level. Some are helpful to students (such as dictionaries or language translators), some are helpful for instructors (such as online syllabi), and others provide material about the Internet's role in marketing. We'd like to share some of our favorites with you:

- Guide to search engines: www.searchenginewatch.com
- Fondren Library search strategies: www.rice.edu/Fondren/Netguides/strategies.html
- Webster's dictionary and thesaurus: www.m-w.com/dictionary.htm
- Bartlett's quotations: http://www.bartleby.com/99/
- AltaVista's Babelfish language translator: http://babelfish.altavista.digital.com
- Research it one-stop reference desk: www.itools.com/research-it/

- Directions and map to anywhere (Zip2): www.zip2.com
- List of e-mail lists (Liszt): www.liszt.com
- Free discussion list hosting (ListBot): www.listbot.com
- Access to Usenet and tens of thousands of discussion groups: www.deja.com
- IBM's product evaluation for online marketing: advisor.internet.ibm.com/inet.nsf/eye?openForm
- UT Austin advertising links: advertising.utexas.edu/world
- Marketing on the Internet syllabi and projects: www.prenhall.com/frost
- Best business-to-business Web sites: www.netb2b.com/nm200

Workbook Evolution

The authors have been teaching Internet Marketing courses continuously since 1995. Over time we have refined this guide as a complement to an introductory principles of marketing text. The authors, residing in two departments (management information systems and marketing), bring a rich interdisciplinary perspective in order to understand the important developments in Internet Marketing.

The text and exercises in *Prentice Hall's e-Marketing Guide* have changed significantly since the first edition of this workbook. As the Net evolves, we incorporate new material and more challenging exercises while maintaining the overall structure. We capitalize on new developments such as online auctions and shopping agents. We appreciate any feedback from workbook users that will help us to keep the book up-to-date and useful for students.

We have also developed an upper level text, *e-Marketing* (formerly *Marketing on the Internet*), for a stand alone course on Internet Marketing. *e-Marketing* is now in its second edition and is available from Prentice-Hall.

About the Authors

Raymond Frost and Judy Strauss have collaborated on many Web-based projects. They have developed many Web sites since 1995, and published academic papers on issues of Web audience measurement, Internet survey research, consumer/company e-mail communication, and Internet pedagogy. In addition, they conduct e-Marketing and Web site development training seminars for business clients. Their comprehensive textbook entitled *e-Marketing* is in its second edition and is available from Prentice-Hall. An online instructor's manual accompanies the book (www.prenhall.com/frost).

Raymond Frost is Professor of Management Information Systems at Ohio University. He has published scholarly papers on database management and is an associate editor of *The Journal of Database Management*. Frost has ten years of experience managing university computer laboratories. He currently teaches e-commerce, database and interdisciplinary courses. Frost earned a doctorate in business administration and an MS in computer science at the University of Miami, and received his BA in philosophy at Swarthmore College. Contact: frostr@ohiou.edu

Judy Strauss is Assistant Professor of Marketing at University of Nevada, Reno. She has published academic papers in electronic marketing, advertising and marketing education. She has had many years of professional experience in marketing, serving as entrepreneur as well as marketing director of two firms. She currently teaches business on the Web, introductory marketing courses at both the undergraduate and MBA level, and marketing communications. Strauss earned a doctorate in marketing at Southern Illinois University, and a finance MBA and marketing BBA at University of North Texas. Contact: jstrauss@unr.edu

Dedications

To our students who make teaching its own reward

Judy
To my daughters—Cyndi and Malia

Raymond
To my son—Raymond Edward Frost

Marketing in the 21ˢᵗ Century

It's all about the customer. In the 21ˢᵗ century, customers want everything more quickly, easily, and value laden than ever before. And they have the power to get it. The days of marketers holding consumers captive for 30 seconds in front of a TV screen are quickly coming to a close. The Web is training individuals and corporate customers to help themselves to information, products, and virtually everything they want anytime, and anywhere. Marketers must study consumer and business needs in the online environment and figure out how to meet these needs better than competitors. Then they can design a marketing mix that provides value. During the process, marketers must figure out which customers are profitable, which to attract, and which to retain. Internet technologies make all of this possible in ways previously thought unimaginable. For example, American Airlines knows a lot about the needs and characteristics its heaviest users: the frequent flyers. Based on this information, American provides password protected account information on the Web and special incoming 1-800 telephone numbers to members of its AllAdvantage club. When a frequent flyer logs onto the Web site to search for flights, American automatically uses the member's closest airport as the trip starting point. For prospects as well as current customers, American provides weekly e-mail notification of specially priced trips to over 1.7 million individuals in its database. And that's not all: American Airlines partner MCI sends customers monthly e-mail notes with frequent flyer mileage earned from long distance.

American Airlines identified many social trends and changing values in the U.S. culture when it designed Internet services for customers and prospects. The following generalizations can be made about individual and business customers at the beginning of the 21ˢᵗ century:

- **Value** is king. Customers and prospects are one click away from competitors if marketing offers do not provide good cost/benefit ratios. Part of value includes exceeding customer expectations when using products or delivering services. As one time-proven marketing adage suggests, "Under promise and over deliver."

- **Price** is the most important factor for some customers, but not all. Many will gladly pay a premium to purchase from an online firm with which they have had good experiences or one with a trustworthy brand name. Further, extra services often command premium prices.

- **Customization** adds value. Firms such as Yahoo! that provide custom Web pages for users, or Dell Computer Corporation that allow customers to configure products to specification provide flexibility at a low cost.

- **Speed** is everything. Users want to find relevant information and product quickly and receive purchased goods tomorrow. Customers don't want to spend time looking up passwords to enter Web sites or helping firms correct account errors through repeated communication.

- **Convenience** is critical for busy people. They want to shop or pay bills anytime of the day or night, 24/7, and to receive deliveries when convenient for them, not the firm or package delivery service.

- **Easy** does it. Users have enough problems without having to learn special software or run through elaborate instructions simply to order from a Web site or pay bills online. Suppliers can assist businesses with complex installations by providing good customer support.

- **Personalization** makes users feel important, especially when a computer sits between them and the company. Web sites that greet users by name, providing personalized information, Web pages designed for business customers, marketing offers and promotions tailored to user needs, and e-mail addressing specific questions are all ways that marketers personalize in an impersonal computer networked environment. Furthermore, customers want companies to act like they are important to the firm, especially if they are loyal and place large orders.

- **One-stop shopping and integrated solutions** save people time and make life easier. Microsoft gained a huge following when it integrated word processing, spread sheet, and presentation software all in one package. Similarly, Yahoo! And other Internet portals attempt to serve all user information and product needs at one site.

- **Self-service** saves time. Customers want to log on, find information, make purchases, track package shipments, check their accounts, and make inquiries anytime, 24/7. Furthermore, they want to do this on a computer via e-mail or the Web, or on a telephone, PalmPilot, or FAX machine. Naturally they want all methods to produce identical information.

All of this adds up to one new marketing truth for the information age: The power is now in the hands of the person who holds the mouse. Consumers and business buyers alike have 24/7 instant access to information and products, and are literally one click away from doing business with a firm's competitor. This puts a lot of pressure on firms to meet user needs. Naturally, there are many ways to build customer loyalty, and sometimes switching costs are high, however, pre-Internet it was much more difficult to consider competitive offerings on a worldwide basis.

It's Bigger Than the Web

e-Marketers use the Internet to deliver customer value through many digital devices. It is important to realize that the Web is only one of many ways to communicate with users via digital information. The key is to learn which devices a firm's customers and prospects own and prefer to use for various purposes from communication through purchase and post-purchase service. Firms send data via the Internet to customers over a variety of digital devices such as the Web, e-mail, cell phone, or an electronic pager, and receive information from product bar code scanners in grocery stores, e-mail, FAX machines, Web TV, voice mail, and a myriad of other devices. Virtually anything that can send or receive electronic data over the Internet is part of e-Marketing. Putting it all together in easily accessible databases to drive profitability is one huge challenge facing marketers today. In fact, one view of the Internet's future holds that Web pages may become increasingly unimportant in favor of smaller bits of information sent to user wireless devices. For example, users can now access stock prices, Federal Express tracking information, airline flight schedule changes, weather, and more over their cell phone, pager, or PalmPilot devices while in a taxi on the way to a client meeting or the airport. When considering the poor telephone infrastructures in many countries, these wireless devices become even more important.

This *Prentice Hall's e-Marketing Guide* focuses on the Web to demonstrate many marketing uses of the Internet. As you work though the exercises, remember that a lot of things are going on in the background at the firms sponsoring featured Web sites, and that many of the things you see can be viewed on other digital information appliances.

How do Marketers Use the Internet?

The Internet is firmly established as a new marketing tool. Content providers offer valuable information to assist marketing planners. The Net has become an integral piece of the marketing mix, spawning new products and serving both as a distribution channel and a promotional medium for marketing communication. This is how marketers use the Net today, but with changing technology, the future is filled with potential! The following sections outline some important uses of the Internet. The rest of this Guide will take you through more explanation and exercises to experience some of these things for yourself.

Net as Research Tool

Marketers use the Internet to gather data for marketing planning. The Net is similar to the library because much data exists on computers connected to the Net. These data help marketers understand competitors, consumers, the economic environment, political and legal factors, technological forces, and other factors in the macroenvironment affecting an organization. Secondary data on the Net are often more current than published data, and they are easy, inexpensive, and quick to access. However, because anyone can be a content provider, you should always do a quality check on Internet data. Marketing planners also use the Net to collect primary data about consumers. Through online e-mail and Web surveys, Web site registration, and observation of Net user discussions, marketers learn about both current and prospective customers. Finally, marketers use bar code scanners in retail stores, Web site logs, and many other electronic methods to collect customer data for marketing planning.

Products on the Net

One is constantly amazed by the creative products developed for this new medium. First there were the directories and search engines such as Yahoo!, Lycos, AltaVista, and Excite. Then there were products that would help a site be recognized by the search engines. Now products and services include online stock trading, ticket buying, classified ads, auctions, streaming audio and video, games, encryption services, payment services, and auditing services, among others. There are even services called "shopping agents" to help you find the right product at the right price!

Existing firms have also modified current products for online distribution, or offered current products for sale through their Web sites. For example, *Time* magazine puts selected content in its online version, and CD's and book retailers simply use the Internet as a new distribution channel.

Pricing on the Net

Online pricing is a concern for marketers. This is true because many factors create downward pressure on prices. Some of these factors include:

- Shopping agents allow consumers to quickly compare prices for products offered by many online retailers
- As with catalog retailing, consumers do not pay state tax on items shipped from firms doing business in another state

- The costs of online retailing are significantly lower than with brick and mortar stores because of reduced order processing, overhead, inventory, customer service, printing, and mailing costs

The picture is not entirely rosy, however. Increased promotion and distribution costs, along with Web site development and maintenance expenses, both work to increase online pricing. Also, a growing trend is price negotiation online. Auctions are a good example of this. Prior to establishing an online business, firms must complete careful ROI and other profit analyses. Most online firms are not currently profitable, however, but exercise low pricing to "buy" market share for the days when online profits exist for the survivors.

Net as Distribution Channel

The Web is a place for online retailing, also called "e-tailing." Consumers buy automobiles, books, flowers, and just about everything online. Businesses also buy online. In fact 70% of all online sales occur in the business to business market. With e-tailing, the Net resembles a direct mail catalog such as the one you receive from J. Crew or the Sharper Image. Four major differences are:

- **Cost savings**—the firm saves catalog printing and mailing costs. Additionally the retailer saves order entry costs since you are doing the order entry for them!
- **Pull vs. push**—the users actively look for the retailer rather than passively viewing whatever catalogs turn up in the mailbox.
- **Payment concerns**—some users are still more worried about giving their credit card over the Net than over the telephone—though this is changing rapidly.
- **Information overload**—currently the biggest concern for online shoppers is finding the right products online. Shopping agents help, but until the Web becomes better organized this problem will continue to plague shoppers.

Online retailers must develop the following services before opening their virtual doors: Web store design and hosting, order processing, order fulfillment, credit authorization, inventory management, merchandising, data warehousing and mining, and customer service.

The Net is also a medium to distribute digital products. Software can be downloaded directly from the Net for free or for fee (e.g., shareware). Electronic magazines, music and video are also distributed directly over the Net, straight to your computer desktop. These activities reduce the number of intermediaries, thus shortening the distribution channel and significantly cutting an organization's costs.

The Net also helps businesses in the distribution channel to collaborate in mutually beneficial ways. For example the bookseller, Amazon.com, has thousands of associates: these are other Web sites that receive up to a 15% commission for referring their users to Amazon for online book purchases. Electronic Data Systems (EDS), the information services company, uses a private computer network, called an extranet or corporate portal, for communication about products and activities with its distribution channel partners.

Net as Communication Medium

The Net is a strong medium for communication with target audiences. In fact, many believe that this function, along with product distribution functions (e-commerce), are the Net's main benefits to marketers. In this function the Net is similar to a magazine or television except that the Net allows two-way communication. Organizations use the Web for the promotional purposes of advertising, sales promotion, direct marketing, and public relations. Some specific uses are:

- **Public relations**—Maintain a Web site with information about products and services ("brochureware"), hold online events, and communicate with a number of different stakeholders
- **Advertising**—Purchase advertising banners, buttons, and sponsorships on other people's Web sites
- **Direct marketing**—Build e-mail databases of consumers for communication purposes, and personalize Web pages and advertising banners for individual users
- **Sales promotions**—Offer electronic coupons, hold sweepstakes, distribute free samples of music and software, and conduct other online sales promotions

Get ready for an exciting hands-on exploration of the Internet and its many marketing uses! Along the way, remember the most important rule of e-Marketing: The rules are constantly changing.

Why are there Mistakes in this Book?

They changed their Web site, that's why! We created an exercise on a weekend and gave it to our classes on Monday, only to find it didn't work as planned. The home page we used had changed and our instructions suddenly became difficult to follow. This *will* happen to you somewhere in this book. So, what should you do?

One thing that might help is to understand the path system used in Web page naming. If we send you to the site, www.cc.gatech.edu/gvu/user_surveys, and it is no longer there, what should you do? The first part (www.cc.gatech.edu) identifies the host computer at that site. All pages at the site are contained in folders (subdirectories) of the host computer. For example, the information that you need is in the gvu/user_surveys folder. Fortunately, you rarely need to know in which subdirectory the information you are searching for is contained. A well-designed site will have a home page on the host computer at the top level (www.cc.gatech.edu) with links to all the pages on the site. So if www.cc.gatech.edu/gvu/user_surveys is not bringing you the information that you require, then simply back up to www.cc.gatech.edu and work your way to the information by following the links.

Another thing to remember is that there are many sources for some types of information. If something changes, try using the search engines to find another source that will answer the questions. This will really increase your surfing skills.

By the way, this feature of change is good. Content providers can continually update their pages and change graphics to keep them useful, without bearing the heavy costs of printed materials. They can experiment with new ideas at low cost and keep things fresh so consumers will be enticed to return.

Chapter **1**

Search Strategies

Estimated time: 105 minutes

Chapter Outline

- Search Overview
    Start in the Right Place
    Internet Portals
- Directory Search
- Keyword Search
    Pluses and Minuses
    Combining Functions
    When in Doubt, Use Lowercase
    A Star for the Wildcard
    Who is Linked to Us?
- Leveraging Technology
    How Search Engines Work

Learning Objectives

- Engage in directory and keyword searches using a Web portal
- Evaluate appropriate uses of a directory vs. a keyword search
- Understand the function of cross-listing
- Refine a search by including and excluding search words
- Use wildcard operators to broaden a search
- Refine a search by using quotation marks to force search words to appear together
- Construct a search which finds sites linking to another site

Search Overview

Searching for information on the Internet is a bit like wandering into a very large library. If you know what you are doing you can locate information rather quickly. If you wander around aimlessly you can get distracted for hours. And while the aimless experience may be enjoyable, you won't get any closer to finishing your research. As in the library, half the battle on the Internet is starting in the right place—the other half of the battle is using the search tool effectively. Most Internet users start in the same place every time—typically one of the major Web portals such as Yahoo!, Lycos, Excite, AltaVista, Infoseek, or Hotbot. Unfortunately, many Internet users do not utilize the sophisticated search options that these sites offer. Typical users will visit Yahoo!, type their search term in the search box and then see what happens. Sound familiar? This exercise will open doors to some more sophisticated search sites and techniques. Enjoy the ride!

Start in the Right Place

With each passing year more information is online. This is particularly good news for students who tend to prefer Internet research to library research. Many school libraries have accepted this new reality and now place many of their databases online so that students can access them over the Web. If you are particularly fortunate, your school even provides access to full text journal articles online. However, beware that not everything is online. You still may have to hoof it over to the library to do some serious research. Also remember that professors tend to look more favorably on papers that demonstrate library research. Why? Because the library references have some editorial control. Many eyes have proofread almost every item in the library collection. The content of library items is edited many times prior to publication and not everything gets published. The reason library resources are edited is pure economics. Publishing on paper is expensive—firms don't want to publish unless they know people will buy. Because people prefer buying good quality, editorial control becomes important. However, on the Internet publishing is free. There is no economic motivation for editorial control. Anyone can put up a Web page with ridiculous claims. But if you cite these lame sources in your paper, then what does that say about the value of your paper? Exactly. But don't lose heart—the Internet is still a great place to do research. You just have to find the right sites and then carefully evaluate the quality of the information that you retrieve.

Starting in the right place online depends on what you are looking for. All of the major search engines index large portions of the Web, though they use varying techniques to do so. What you are after is relevance. What is the most relevant site to answer your research question? The search engines go to great trouble to produce relevant listings but they aren't always on target. This is where knowing a few good sites can pay big dividends. In general, if you can figure out who might have a reason to publish the data you need, that is a good place to start. The following guide should help:

To Search For	Try
Encyclopedia articles	www.encyclopedia.com
	www.ask.com (accepts natural language)
Online Almanac	www.infoplease.com
General News Stories	wire.ap.org (AP Newswire)
	dailynews.yahoo.com (Yahoo! News Archives)
	nt.excite.com (Newstracker)
Geographically Targeted New Stories	www.newstrawler.com (Newstrawler)
	emedia1.mediainfo.com/emedia/ (Media Info)
Newsgroups talking about a particular subject	www.talkway.com (Talkway)
	www.deja.com (Deja)
The FAQs (frequently asked questions and answers) which most newsgroups and e-mail mailing lists provide for new users.	www.faqs.org (Internet FAQ consortium)
Mailing list directories on every conceivable subject	www.liszt.com (Liszt, the mailing list directory)
Photographs and other graphic images	www.AltaVista.com (Photo & Media Finder)
	ipix.yahoo.com (Yahoo! image surfer)
Audio & Video clips and live broadcasts	mp3.lycos.com (MP3 Search)
	realguide.real.com (RealGuide)
	broadcast.com (Yahoo! Broadcast)
People's e-mail or phone numbers	people.yahoo.com
Yellow Pages	yp.yahoo.com
Maps	maps.yahoo.com

Exhibit 1 - 1 Yahoo! Portal and Search Directory
Source: www.yahoo.com Reproduced with permission of Yahoo! Inc. Copyright © 2000 by Yahoo! Inc. YAHOO! And the YAHOO! logo are trademarks of Yahoo! Inc.

Internet Portals

An Internet portal is a Web site so useful that many people make it their homepage or point of entry to the rest of the Internet. The major portals include Yahoo.com, aol.com, msn.com, go.com, netscape.com, excite.com, lycos.com, and AltaVista.com. These portals earn revenue by attracting visitors and selling ads. The more eyeballs they attract, the more they can charge for their ad inventory. Portals also try to enhance their stickiness—the amount of time that users spend on the site—by offering a wide variety of services. Nonetheless, most users start at Web portals because of the directory and search services.

Virtually all of the Internet portals offer two types of searches: keyword search and directory search. A keyword search is like using the index in a book, whereas a directory search is like using the table of contents. Keyword searches look for a word or group of words that were entered as a search string. Directory searches require the user to navigate through categories and subcategories. In this chapter we will look at the Yahoo! and AltaVista portals. Yahoo! is best known for its directory whereas AltaVista is best known for its keyword search.

Directory Search

A Web directory is an index of a great number of pages on the Web, neatly organized by category, sub-category, sub-sub-category, and so forth. For example:

Recreation ➔ Automotive ➔ Makes and Models ➔ Porsche

Users navigate down through the directory until they reach a link pointing to a page that looks relevant. Directory navigation takes effort but the results are often very relevant to the information needs.

For efficient searching, it is helpful to understand how the people at Yahoo! create their directory. Their home page lists 14 general categories, under which all their catalogued Web sites are listed. A search begins with a general topic and "drills down" to increasingly specific topics. When assigning sites to categories, Yahoo! considers:

- Commercial versus non-commercial. **All** sites about companies that sell products are listed under Business and Economy ➔ Companies. These same sites are probably cross-listed somewhere else as well, just to make things easier for you. For example, a company selling music CD's will also be listed under Entertainment ➔ Music.

- Regional versus non-regional. An increasing number of Web sites target local audiences. Yahoo! lists **all** local sites under Regional so if you are looking for hotels in San Francisco you know where to begin searching. If a company is truly global, such as Apple Computer, it will not be in the regional listings.

You may see some entries followed by an @ symbol, such as Advertising on Web and Internet@. The @ sign means that this category is cross-listed under another heading. It is helpful to understand that sites are cross-listed and that in a good directory you can find what you want using several different approaches.

The following exercise has you navigate Yahoo!'s directory both manually in a drill down fashion and also by using the search box feature. To get to Yahoo!'s site simply type: www.yahoo.com in the address line of your browser and then press the return key. (Hint: typing yahoo only works also as most browsers automatically add the www prefix and the .com suffix.)

1. Manual navigation through a directory is especially useful when you are exploring in a less focused fashion. Let's assume that your professor assigns a term paper on a marketing topic of your choice. Use the Yahoo! directory to look for a topic starting with Business and Economy ➔ Marketing. What topic did you choose? (write down the complete path to the topic using the same notation as the Porsche example above)

2. Now let's imagine that you have a Web site to promote and you would like to retrieve a list of companies that can help you promote your Web site. Promotion is part of the marketing mix so we begin again with Business and Economy ➔ Marketing. Continue on until you find a list of site promotion pages and write the full path here.

3. Now return to Yahoo!'s home page and try the same search for promotion using the search box. What search term did you type? Did it bring you to the same place?

4. You will want to use the search box when you don't know in which category to look for a given subject. Your success with the search box feature will to a large extent depend on how specific you can be with the search term. Using the Yahoo! search feature, conduct the three searches in the following table, progressively narrowing down a subject. Record the number of matches encountered with each search string.

Keywords Searched for	Number of Yahoo! category matches	Number of Yahoo! site matches
coupons		
food coupons		
grocery food coupons		

What conclusion can be drawn from this experiment?

5. The number in parentheses after a category indicates how many listings are in that category. For example, click on Business and Economy ➜ Marketing and record here the number of listings under Anti-telemarketing.

6. Now we'd like you to try looking for your hometown newspaper by starting at three different general categories on Yahoo!'s home page. This exercise will demonstrate that there are many ways to find a Web site. For each search, write the path you took:

   i.

   ii.

   iii.

7. Yahoo! uses 14 top level categories to organize its directory. The categorization scheme is an invention of Yahoo!'s. This is unlike the library. Years ago libraries across the country standardized on the Dewey decimal system. This way no matter which library you enter you will find the same books in the same section of the library. By contrast, there is no universal categorization scheme for the Internet. Each portal carves up the world as it sees fit. Nonetheless, there does tend to be some

uniformity among schemes. Let's compare Yahoo!'s way of organizing the world to that employed by some of its competitors. For each competitor write down the top level category which corresponds to Yahoo!'s. If the competitor has a top level category which does not correspond to Yahoo!'s, then enter that category on one of the blank lines at the end of the table.

Yahoo!	Excite	Lycos	Go
Arts & Humanities			
Business & Economy			
Computers & Internet			
Education			
Entertainment			
Government			
Health			
News & Media			
Recreation & Sports			
Reference			
Regional			
Science			
Social Science			
Society & Culture			

8.   What can you conclude about the target audiences of the various sites based on their choices of top level categories?

Exhibit 1 - 2 AltaVista Search Engine
Source: www.altavista.com

Keyword Search

The last exercise introduced the Yahoo! directory. The Yahoo! directory contains all of the pages that the Yahoo! editors have had time to categorize. And while they have categorized a lot, the Yahoo! directory is far from complete. By contrast, AltaVista uses a spider program to search the Web and index documents by keywords. As a result AltaVista has a great deal more of the Web covered in its database, but still far from all of it. There are a number of spider based search engines like AltaVista. The reason there are so many keyword search engines is that spider software is cheap whereas human labor is expensive. Because spiders work tirelessly day and night, they are able to visit millions of pages on the Web and index all the keywords that they find on those pages.

Following are just a few important tips for using the search tools more effectively. Using the "help" button is the most important thing to remember. Also, in general do not use capital letters; lowercase matches both lower and uppercase whereas uppercase matches uppercase only. However, if you are looking for the country "Turkey," do use a capital letter to exclude the bird "turkey" from search results. For keyword searches:

- Use quotation marks (e.g., "Internet course") to indicate words that must be right next to each other—otherwise the search engine will turn up pages where the two words appear separated on the page.

- Be careful in selecting words and be as specific as possible. The word "butterfly" will retrieve sites about the insect as well as swimming.

- If a search reveals too many unrelated listings, simply use additional words to qualify the original term— get increasingly specific. You can even try full sentences on most search engines.

- Use a plus when the word should appear in the text and a minus when you want text without that word appearing (e.g., + "internet course" – university).

Pluses and Minuses

Searching the Web means being able to specify wanted and unwanted search results. In AltaVista a plus means that you want the word to appear on a Web page, and a minus means that you don't. So +pizza -beer gives you all sites that have pizza but no beer. On the other hand -pizza +beer gives you all sites that have no pizza but lots of beer. Ready? Start up AltaVista by entering its address in your Web browser—www.altavista.com. You should see a welcome page.

9.   Enter a search string in the box and then click the search button. Let's try our pizza and beer example. Be sure to include a space between the words, or AltaVista will think you are searching for one long word.

You Type	It Means
+pizza -beer	Find all pages that have lots of pizza but no beer

About how many documents were returned by the query?

10. Are you going to read them all? We didn't think so. Now try the second example.

You Type	It Means
-pizza +beer	Find all pages that have no pizza but lots of beer

About how many documents were returned by the query?

As you can see, with over 250 million pages covered on the Web, AltaVista is going to find a lot of stuff. Some of it will be right on target but most of it will be junk. Luckily, AltaVista tries to position the most relevant documents at the top of the list. So how does it determine what's relevant? This is actually a trade secret. However, most search engines look first at where the keywords appear in a Web page. Words appearing in the title or towards the top of the page are weighted more heavily. Search engines also look at the frequency with which the words appear.

A cottage industry has grown up including companies such as www.webposition.com and www.did-it.com who investigate how the search engines perform their rankings and then help you engineer your pages to achieve the highest possible relevance ranking. Bottom line—you can pay to get noticed.

Combining Functions

11. Sometimes you want search terms to appear right next to each other with no words in between. To accomplish this we put the words in quotes. Let's say we are interested in pages on **web marketing**. We'll get better results by entering the search string **"web marketing"**. But what if we want to limit it further to just those sites that mention the Nielsen Survey? Try it yourself and see what you get.

You Type	It Means
+"web marketing" +"nielsen survey"	Find all pages that have the words web and marketing where those words appear right next to each other. Those same sites must also have the words nielsen and survey right next to each other.

About how many documents were returned by the query?

You can get very specific! Now try some on your own. For each of the following questions write down the query that you would type in the search box.

12. Find Web sites about Honda motorcycles which do not mention automobiles or cars.

13. Find Web sites about the White House which do not mention Clinton.

14. Find Web sites about apples which do not mention music, computers or the Macintosh

When in Doubt, Use Lowercase

You may have noticed that in all of the examples above, the search strings were typed in lowercase even when searching for a proper name such as Nielsen. The reason for this is that lowercase matches both lower and uppercase whereas uppercase matches uppercase only. So, if some Webmaster forgets to capitalize Nielsen, you'll still find that site.

A Star for the Wildcard

15. What if you are looking for information on **European** Travel Agents? It is reasonable to assume that **Europe** Travel Agent would also produce a good match. Rather than running two searches we can use the wildcard notation to match all words that start with **Europe** (i.e., **Europe**an) by typing **europe***. Try the following example:

You Type	It Means
+europe* +"travel agent"	Find all pages that have words that begin with europe. Those same pages must have the words travel agent right next to each other

About how many documents were returned by the query?

Who is Linked to Us?

On the Web, more is better when it comes to site visitors: More visitors create more potential business and/or more ability to sell ads. Visitors can locate a site in many ways:

1. by deducing or guessing a site name, for example, www.coca-cola.com
2. by searching for the site using a search engine,
3. by copying the address from an advertisement or other media, or
4. by following a "hot link" from another site.

Interestingly, Coopers and Lybrand Consulting found that 39% of Web users learn about sites through other media, 44% through word-of-mouth, 32% through browsing, and 10% through "hot links" (source: www.cyberatlas.com).

16. At some point in your marketing studies your professor will ask you to research demographics. One good source of demographics is American Demographics magazine at www.demographics.com. However, other good sources of information might include any site which sets a link to American Demographics. You can get a list of these sites by using the AltaVista link operator.

You Type	It Means
link:www.demographics.com	Find all pages with a **link** to American Demographics

How many sites link to American Demographics?

17. List three sites that link to American Demographics and look like good research leads.

18. Write the search query to find how many sites link to the Census Bureau at www.census.gov.

Interestingly, some search engines actually use the number of links to a site to help compute its relevancy ranking. Not a bad idea since the Web community is effectively voting with its links. Another search engine, Hotbot, ranks sites by how many users visit the site and how long they stay. Some engines, such as google.com, use a feature called "Direct Hit" that measures the popularity of a site to determine its importance. See the Leveraging Technology below for more information.

By the way, links from other sites are not always welcome. Ticketmaster at one time sued Microsoft for providing a link to their site. Their gripe? The Microsoft link did not point to their home page but rather to a subpage. Ticketmaster wants to communicate with users through the "front door" perhaps so that they will see a full menu of products, promotions, and advertising.

Leveraging Technology

How Search Engines Work

The Web is a very big place with hundreds of millions of pages. Realistically it would be impossible for the search engines to search the entire Web every time someone types in a search term. It would take days to complete the task. So what do search engines do? They actually do the searching up to a month in advance and then store the results in a huge database. They send automatic programs called spiders out on the Web to go from site to site, page by page and word by word. See Exhibit 1 - 3. These spiders build up a massive index or database of all the words found, where they were found, how many times they appear on each page, etc. It is this database which is actually queried when you type in a search term. Because it is an indexed database the query returns the results almost instantly. The results are generally returned in order of reievance with the most relevant site appearing first. But how do they know? It is the search engine's job to figure out which sites are most likely to be relevant to your search term. Here the spider aids it. The spider does more than just count words. It also looks for the location of those words on the page. For example, if the word is in the title of a page then it is given a higher relevance value than a word appearing in the body text. The spiders are also trained to avoid sites that attempt to trick them by repeating words more often. One technique is to ignore repeats that are not separated by at least, say, seven other words. This guards against someone loading their site with, for example, Mazda, Mazda, Mazda. The actual techniques used are becoming trade secrets since producing a search engine that returns truly useful results is actually a point of product differentiation and therefore provides a competitive advantage. Nonetheless, one Web site, searchenginewatch.com, reveals many of the secrets for each of the search engines.

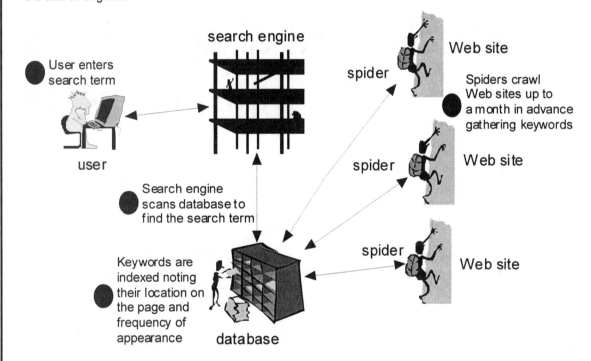

Exhibit 1 - 3 How Search Engines Work

Two search engines break from the mold in that they rely on user behavior to form their rankings. Google (www.google.com) ranks sites according to how many links point to the site from other Web sites. A popular site should have more links pointing to it than one that is less popular. DirectHit (www.directhit.com) ranks sites according to how frequently users chose that site when presented with search results. A site which is chosen more often should be the more relevant site.

Chapter 2

Market Analysis Using Secondary Data

Estimated time: 105 minutes

Chapter Outline

- The Net for Secondary Data
  Environmental Scan

- Toyota Echo
  Demographics
  Cultural Trends
  Competition
  Deja.com
  Putting It All Together

- Leveraging Technology
  Measuring Web Site Traffic

Learning Objectives

- Apply appropriate search strategies to find information quickly on the Web

- Explore Web sites with information about the macroenvironment

- Understand newsgroups as a source of competitive intelligence

The Net for Secondary Data

Any computer connected to the Internet is like a book sitting on a library shelf. It is there to be accessed and used as a source of information. A major difference is that the information available on the Internet is not censored, reviewed, or authorized by anyone other than the owner of the computer. The information is also manageable; it can be changed and updated at any moment. This, of course, leads to a great number of Web sites containing information of questionable quality. Nonetheless, there are many ways that the Internet is better than the library. It is open 24 hours a day, the information is often more current, and users have equal access from all over the world. This information is also quick to find, easy to download to your computer, and there are no fines or late fees (as long as you don't break copyright law!).

It is important to remember that the library and other secondary data sources contain lots of information that is not available on the Internet. A good researcher will explore many information sources and then compare data for accuracy and appropriateness before making decisions.

What types of information do marketing managers need that might be available on the Net? It is important to collect information about consumers, competition, and other factors outside of the organization. These data help to answer the question: What opportunities and threats are in the business environment for a particular organization and industry? Armed with this knowledge, marketing managers can plan products, pricing, distribution, and promotion that better meet the needs of organizations and individuals.

In this chapter we focus on secondary data: information gathered by someone else who makes it available to us. Sources of secondary data on the Internet vary from the U.S. Census Bureau to online magazines and research companies that provide statistics and analyses to help marketers make decisions.

Environmental Scan

To identify threats and opportunities, a corporation wants information about the macroenvironment in which it operates. An environmental scan seeks market information about the following:

- **Demographic trends**—Population characteristics such as age, income, and education

- **Social and cultural trends**—Changing values and habits such as health consciousness and time poverty

- **Competitors**—Brands that fulfill similar needs in the same market

- **Technological forces**—Innovations outside an industry that can be applied to both products and processes, such as the Internet and laser technology

- **Resource availability**—Land, labor, and capital availability

- **Economics**— Business cycles and changes in income and spending patterns

- **Legal and political environments**— Political leaders and legislation affecting particular industries

Much of this information is available on the Internet: some for free, and some for a fee. The Toyota Echo exercise will guide you to many sources of free information. Remember to evaluate it by determining its source, timeliness and general quality.

Toyota Echo

Automobile manufacturers are continually seeking information about changes in the automobile industry and its macroenvironment. This exercise focuses on the Toyota Company (www.toyota.com) and directs you to perform an environmental scan on their behalf as they gauge a new product introduction. The product is the Toyota Echo, actually introduced in fall 1999. It is a low price, high quality vehicle made for car buyers who are 18-33 years of age.

Demographics

Is there a large target college population for the Echo? An excellent source of demographic information on the Web is the U.S. Census site. Like many government Web sites it is free and maintained by your tax dollars. Maybe they should sell advertising! While the official census takes place every 10 years, the Census Bureau maintains more current statistics from other surveys. We will use the Census statistics to study the size and composition of the college market. Locate the U.S. Census Web site at www.census.gov. You should see a screen that looks similar to Exhibit 2 - 1.

At the Census site, click on *subjects A-Z*. Next find *College Enrollment*. Under "Historical Tables" click on *Table A-7: College Enrollment of Students 14 to 34 Years Old*. This information will help you advise Toyota on the attractiveness of the college student target market. Remember what we said earlier about Web sites constantly changing? If these instructions don't take you to this particular table, you can follow your nose through the new site to find the information for this exercise.

1.   How many undergraduate students in this age group were enrolled in college during the most current year for which they have information? Caution! The figures listed are in thousands.

2.   Is the trend up or down since the previous year?

3.   Is the market better for female or male students?

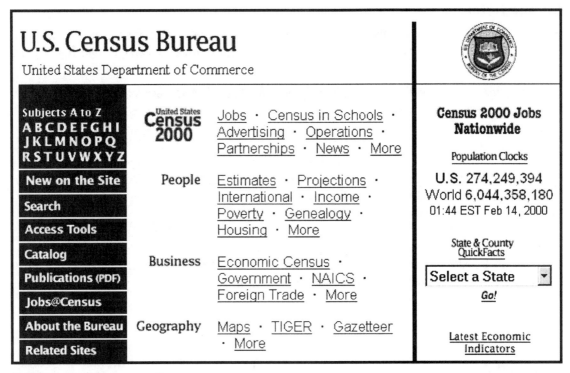

Exhibit 2 - 1 U.S. Census Bureau
Source: www.census.gov

Cultural Trends

How is the market changing? Would the Echo appeal to its target market? Visit American Demographics/Marketing Tools at www.demographics.com and follow the link to *Marketing Tools Magazine.* Conduct a full text search using the term "generation X." Review the articles to learn more about this market and answer the following questions. Be sure to read "The Lost Generation" in the April 1997 issue.

4. What is the spending power for young people on a yearly basis?

5. Briefly describe three values held by Generation X that might affect Toyota's advertising messages.

6. Which media should Toyota use to reach Generation X consumers?

Competition

How does the Echo compare with the competition? Prior to finalizing the marketing strategy, you will assist Toyota in a competitive analysis. Visit the Toyota home page, www.toyota.com and find the Toyota Echo model.

7. Locate the vehicle specifications and write down what basic features are included and how many colors are available.

8. Now find Edmund's automotive home page at www.edmunds.com and find their review of the Toyota Echo. List 3 competitors identified by Edmund's.

9. Look up Edmund's review of one of the competitors you identified above. How does the Echo compare with this competitor (strengths/weaknesses)?

Deja.com

These sites are not the only way for Toyota to learn about competition. They can visit competitor's Web sites, read reviews in online magazines, and they can also check the Usenet. The Usenet consists of over 35,000 news groups, each one a forum for public discussion on a very specific topic. People post articles to newsgroups for others to read. Discussions range from the meaningful to the absurd, but marketing planners can learn about products and industries by monitoring discussions. There are even firms that, for a fee, monitor the Usenet and notify corporations of any bad rumors circulating about them. This gives them an opportunity to quickly post a response to dispel the rumor. You can do some of this sleuthing on your own. A highly specialized search engine called Deja.com has been developed to save and index all postings to the Usenet.

10. Let's taste the flavor of discussion about the Echo competition. Visit the Usenet at Deja.com on the Web at www.deja.com. Toyota would like to know which newsgroups to monitor in the future, so enter one Echo competitor in the discussion search box then click the *Find* button. What are four newsgroups you see listed? Note that Deja.com rates the ones nearer to the top as more relevant to your search.

11. Check out some of the conversation and report on one thing that you learn which would be helpful to Toyota marketing managers.

12. How would this information help Toyota?

Putting It All Together

Now reflect on what you have learned so far to complete the following table. For each item listed, indicate one or more Web sites *not* mentioned in this exercise that provide secondary data for marketing decision making in the automobile industry. Use the search skills from the previous chapter to help out. Then rate each Web site in terms of content and style (the site's look/feel and ease of navigation) on a scale from 1 to 10 with 10 being the highest score.

Trend	Web site name and URL	Content	Style
demographic trends			
Social and cultural trends			
competitors			
technological forces			
economies			
legal and political environments			

Leveraging Technology

Measuring Web Site Traffic

One crucial type of secondary data for Web sites is an analysis of traffic relative to the competition. For television shows, the Nielsen ratings provide these important data to help networks modify their programming and charge for advertising. For Internet ratings, Media Metrix, Nielsen//NetRatings, and @Plan perform the same function.

Nielsen//NetRatings uses a representative panel of over 14,000 of home users. Panel members agree to run software on their computers which will monitor their behavior as they surf the Internet. The software records where they go and how long they stay there. The software also reports back at scheduled intervals to Nielsen//NetRatings where the data are analyzed in the aggregate. Using these data, Nielsen//NetRatings is able to generalize results to the entire population of Web users. On their site you will find a list of the top 10 Web sites ranked by reach percentage. The demographic targeting reports allows users to select the target demographic that interests them and receive a list of sites matching that demographic. See Exhibit 2 - 2 and Exhibit 2 - 3.

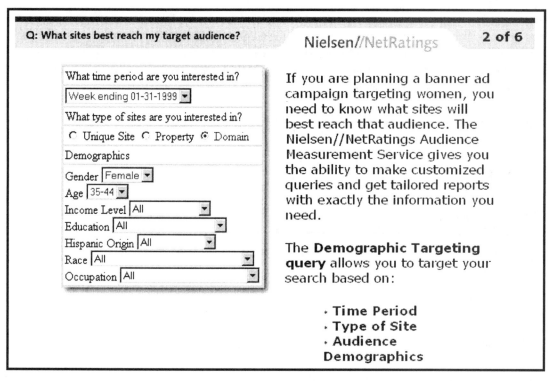

Q: What sites best reach my target audience?   Nielsen//NetRatings   **2 of 6**

What time period are you interested in?
Week ending 01-31-1999

What type of sites are you interested in?
⊙ Unique Site ⊙ Property ⊙ Domain

Demographics

Gender Female
Age 35-44
Income Level All
Education All
Hispanic Origin All
Race All
Occupation All

If you are planning a banner ad campaign targeting women, you need to know what sites will best reach that audience. The Nielsen//NetRatings Audience Measurement Service gives you the ability to make customized queries and get tailored reports with exactly the information you need.

The **Demographic Targeting query** allows you to target your search based on:

- **Time Period**
- **Type of Site**
- **Audience Demographics**

Exhibit 2 - 2 Nielsen//NetRatings Demographic Targeting Query
Source: www.nielsen-netratings.com

Demographic Targeting Report - Females, Ages 35-44

SAVE AS TEXT FILE   QUICK HELP

Site	Unique Audience	Composition %	Composition Index	Coverage %
website_1.com	397,012	75.68	138	2.2
website_2.com	1,488,795	73.94	127	8.25
website_3.com	326,117	62.16	121	1.81
website_4.com	680,592	57.14	100	3.77
website_5.com	255,909	54.55	100	1.42

The result of the query lists the target sites by **composition index**. A composition index of 100 indicates that visitors to a site meet expected or average internet gender proportions. A site with a 138 index has 38% more women than the average site.

Exhibit 2 - 3 Nielsen//NetRatings Demographic Targeting Report
Source: www.nielsen-netratings.com

Other available reports include:

- Web Site Reports by property, domain, site or category

- Bannertrack[sm] Reports by impression, domain, or company

- Audience Summary Reports by profile, or traffic

For these reports to be valid the panel must be statistically representative of the sampled population. After all, they are generalizing the behavior of millions of people based on the actions of thousands. And the stakes are very high since advertisers use the reports as the basis to make ad buys. Because many sites are ad-supported their very livelihood may depend on the reports.

So how does Nielsen//NetRatings generate a representative panel? Most marketers agree that the best way to form a panel is by randomly dialing phone numbers in the geographic area sampled. The reasoning? First, almost everyone owns a telephone. Second, the response rate from a phone call is higher than that obtained through a direct mailing. Basically, people have a harder time turning down a persistent voice.

Chapter 3

Market Analysis Using Primary Data

Estimated time: 60 minutes

Chapter Outline

- Primary Data Collection Online
    Primary Data Collection Procedure
    The Internet as Contact Method
    Ethical Concerns
    Web Registration
- American Consumer Opinion
- Registering at a Web Site
- Learning About a Firm's Web Customers
- Leveraging Technology
    Privacy, Log Files and Cookies

Learning Objectives

- Experience the Web as a medium for primary data collection
- Discuss how traditional research methods can be used on the Internet
- Explain how e-mail can be used for gathering primary data
- Recognize the advantages and limitations of the Net for primary market research
- Understand some of the privacy issues regarding survey research on the Net

Primary Data Collection Online

When secondary data are not available to assist in marketing planning, managers may decide to collect their own information. Primary data is information gathered to solve a particular problem. It is usually more expensive and time-consuming to gather than secondary data, but on the other hand, the data are generally more relevant to the manager's specific problem.

Primary Data Collection Procedure

A primary data collection project includes many steps. Briefly, managers must decide the following things:

- What is the exact problem?
- What is the research plan?
  - *Research approach*. On the basis of the information need, researchers choose from among experiments, focus groups, observation techniques, and survey research.
  - *Sample design*. At this stage researchers select the sample source and number of desired respondents.
  - *Contact method*. Ways to contact the sample include traditional methods such as the telephone, mail, and in-person as well as the Internet.
  - *Instrument design*. If a survey is planned, researchers develop a questionnaire. If the plan calls for an experiment or observations, they develop a protocol to guide the data collection.
  - *Data collection and analysis*. Researchers gather the information according to plan, then analyze the results in light of the original problem.
- How will the data be distributed to decision makers? Research data might be placed in a marketing information system database or might be presented in written or oral form to marketing managers.

The Internet as Contact Method

When companies want to collect primary data from consumers who use the Internet, they might select the Internet as the contact method. Internet primary research could include one or more of the following research approaches:

- **Online experiments**—Experiments attempt to determine cause and effect relationships. One popular use of this approach online is to use different versions of a banner ad and see which one entices the greatest number of users to click through to the sponsoring site.
- **Online focus groups**—Advertising agencies ask a group of 5-10 users to meet in a special chat room for a discussion on a particular topic.
- **Online observations**—Firms observe consumers in Cyberspace to see how they move through a site and how long they stay on a particular page. These actions are all recorded in the Web server log files

and help firms to design better Web sites. Another strong observational technique is to record user chat about products. The Usenet, with its 35,000 special interest bulletin boards is perfect for this type of data collection. You conducted observation research in Chapter 2 when you checked out discussion about Toyota's competition at Deja.com.

- **Online survey research**— This can be done by sending questionnaires to individuals via e-mail, or by posting a survey or other Web form on the company site. A number of Web questionnaire generation tools are on the market. These include EZSurvey for the Internet, MarketSight, Survey Select, Survey Solutions for the Web, WebSurveyor, and Zoomerang.

Primary data collection on the Internet has advantages and disadvantages.

Advantages to gathering information online include:

1. It is fast and inexpensive.
2. There is a diverse, large group of Net users all over the world.
3. Consumers often are more frank in their responses because a computer separates them from the folks asking questions.
4. It is a great way to reach visitors to a company Web site
5. Electronic data are easy to tabulate automatically.

There are many **disadvantages** as well:

1. There is no way to draw a probability sample of all Net users, so the results are not generalizable to the population.
2. It is easy for respondents to answer questions untruthfully or to pose as different people (e.g., the opposite sex).
3. People often make more errors typing than they do writing, thus submitting inaccurate information.
4. With Web surveys, there is little control over who or how many people fill out the questionnaire, or whether some people fill it out more than once.

Some of the survey generation tools mentioned above can help solve some of the problems in #3 and #4.

Ethical Concerns

In addition to these disadvantages, there are some ethical concerns regarding survey research on the Net:

1. It may not be ethical for researchers to observe private online conversations without notifying the users.
2. With e-mail surveys, respondents may be upset at getting "junk" e-mail.
3. Some researchers "harvest" e-mail addresses from newsgroups without permission.
4. Some companies conduct "surveys" for the purpose of building a database for later solicitation.

Web Registration

The previous discussion concerns primary data collection using the Internet as the contact method. We described various techniques a firm may use in lieu of other contact methods such as the telephone or direct mail. A special case of primary data collection occurs at many Web sites when firms ask users to register. For some sites, such as the travel agent Expedia (www.expedia.com), registration is mandatory prior to using the site's services. For other sites, such as Amazon (www.amazon.com), users can browse anonymously, but must register if they want to buy something or access certain services. Web registration is a great way for a firm to collect data about its users, however users don't like to register and will avoid it if they can. If the firm offers incentives, such as giving access to important services or data, users will be more likely to register.

What do firms do with registration data? Once you have an account with a firm such as Amazon, it can track your visits, noting which pages and products you review or buy. This helps them to design more useful pages and to personalize the home page to your specific interests. In addition to building a better relationship with you through customer service, some firms use registration data to report overall user statistics to potential advertisers. If sites can show that their audience matches the advertiser's audience, firms will be more likely to advertise on the site. A growing concern of customers is that firms may sell data about them to direct marketers. The more reputable firms disclose right on their Web site what they will and will not do with customer data. Guarding customer privacy is a huge concern for e-marketers.

In spite of serious shortcomings, the Net can be a useful place to conduct a primary research project. When using primary or secondary data, you must evaluate its quality carefully and apply it accordingly. In the following exercises you will register at a site, write a survey question, and then complete and review several Web-based surveys.

American Consumer Opinion

Decision Analyst, Inc., a Dallas-based marketing research firm maintains an online consumer panel consisting of households all over the world. The purpose? It uses the panel to test products for clients and to answer a few questionnaires a year online. As with most panels, each member receives cash or product incentives for participation. Visit www.acop.com (see Exhibit 3 - 1) and join their panel (you can always quit at any time, but if you stick it out you might get paid!).

1. What are some of the things American Consumer Opinion wants to know about you?

2. How do you think they will use this information once you are a panel member and respond to their surveys?

3. On the second registration screen they ask how you heard about the site and what you think of it. How do you think this information will help them?

Exhibit 3 - 1 American Consumer Opinion Panels
Source: www.acop.com

4. Now go to the "fun" surveys and try a few. After you answer a question and submit your response, the server automatically adds your answer to the database and tells you the overall distribution of answers to each response option. This is what we meant when we said online surveys are easy and fast! Now, think up your own "fun" question and e-mail it to American Consumer Opinion (instructions are currently on the "information" page). Write the question and response categories here. Note: be sure to check back to see how folks are answering your question!

Registering at a Web Site

5. If you haven't already done so, register at Amazon.com. What are some reasons that Amazon wants your e-mail address? Hint: if you gave your e-mail address when registering, you should check your e-mail in-box.

6. Amazon will use your registration information and purchase history for marketing purposes. What are some of the ways Amazon can build relationship with you by using this information? Hint: see Exhibit 3 - 2 .

Exhibit 3 - 2 Amazon Builds Relationships with Customers

Source: www.amazon.com Amazon.com is a registered trademark or trademark of Amazon.com, Inc. in the U.S. and/or other countries. © 2000 by Amazon.com. All rights reserved.

Exhibit 3 - 3 BizRate Evaluates e-Tailers
Source: www.bizrate.com

Learning About a Firm's Web Customers

Just because Amazon.com is the most well-known online bookstore does not mean it is necessarily the best. Barnes and Noble also has a strong entry in this product category. Fortunately, BizRate.com emerged to help online consumers evaluate various online retailers (see Exhibit 3 - 3). Visit the merchant directory at www.bizrate.com and check out the online bookstores.

7. Which bookstore is the most highly rated by customers? The lowest rated?

8. What is Amazon.com's rating by customers and in staff recommendations? How can you explain the different ratings?

9. Before you accept these data as gospel, you might want to evaluate the quality. Describe how BizRate arrives at consumer/shopper ratings of merchants—you'll find this information on their site (currently in the *merchants only* section). Does this seem like a good research methodology to you? Why or why not?

10. Some merchants offer BizRate users rebates of up to 25% for purchases made at their sites. Does the rebate program fit well with BizRate's mission? Why or why not?

Leveraging Technology

Privacy, Log Files and Cookies

Visitors on the Web, like visitors to a sandy beach, leave footprints wherever they go. The footprints are left in two places—on the computer visited and on the user's own computer. The computer visited maintains a log of all computers which visit the site and exactly which pages they see. The log is in the form of a table, which looks similar to this:

Date	Time	Visitor address	Page viewed
1/10/2001	10:30am	Frost1.ohiou.edu	Baking recipes
1/10/2001	10:31am	Frost1.ohiou.edu	Cookies
1/10/2001	10:32am	Frost1.ohiou.edu	Chocolate chip
1/10/2001	10:40am	Frost1.ohiou.edu	Sign off

A real log file records much more data. However, even in our simple example you can tell that the computer frost1.ohiou.edu (presumably belonging to Frost at Ohio University) navigated quickly down to the recipe for chocolate chip cookies and then stayed there for 8 minutes before leaving the site. This type of information collected for thousands of users can tell marketers which pages are popular, who are repeat users, the days and times that the site is most heavily used, and so forth. Note that the log file only identifies the computer. This makes it difficult to monitor user behavior if more than one user uses the computer—as is the case in university computer labs.

The second way to track behavior on the Web is by use of cookies. Cookies are files stored on the user's computer. Each site you visit may write a cookie on your computer. For example suppose you are a repeat visitor to a site that requires a password. The site could authenticate you by looking up your password in a cookie from a previous session. It could also use the cookie to store your purchase choices in an electronic shopping basket prior to checkout. Cookies are more reliable than computer addresses because a computer's address may change every time it is restarted. See Exhibit 3 - 1.

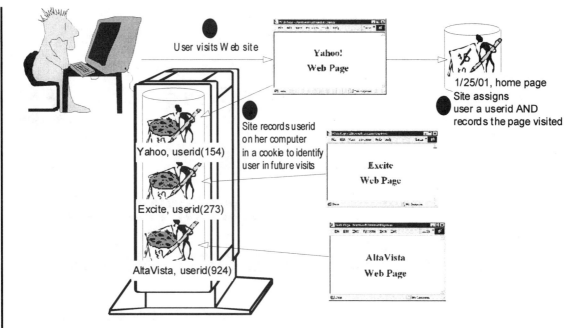

Exhibit 3 - 1 How Cookies are Stored

Both log files and cookies can be helpful to customize products and services to the user community. However, most users do not understand how extensively their behavior is being tracked and this raises a serious question. Is it ethical to gather information about people without their knowledge and explicit consent?

Chapter **4**

Internet User Characteristics and Behavior

Estimated time: 90 minutes

Chapter Outline

- Measuring Eyeballs
  Size and Growth Rate
  Demographics
  Geographics
  Psychographics
  Behavior
  Finding Answers

- Planning an E-zine
  Market Size
  Demographics
  User Behavior
  Geographics
  Psychographics—Stanford Research
  Institute (SRI) VALS
  Putting It All Together

- Leveraging Technology
  Audience Measurement Challenge

Learning Objectives

- Use secondary data to describe the Net audience

- Explore sites that have conducted surveys of Net users

- Apply information about Net users to create a Web magazine

Measuring Eyeballs

The total U.S. Web traffic was greater than 110 million users at the beginning of the year 2000 (source: The Computer Industry Almanac, www.c-i-a.com). The next closest country is Japan with over 18 million users. It is no wonder that the number of businesses displaying their wares on the Web is also growing. While building, designing, and maintaining a site on the Web, however, companies must attempt to understand the characteristics and Net behavior of Net users. Armed with this information, companies can determine if their target markets are in the Net audience, and can further decide how to develop Web sites and new products that attract and appeal to potential customers. While Chapter 3 discussed Web users at individual sites, this chapter focuses on the entire Net population. It is important to note, however, that as the Internet becomes more mainstream the trend is to think less about how many total eyeballs are "out there," and more about how to identify, measure, and describe segments of users for niche marketing.

What specific information do organizations want to know about the audience for this medium?

- Size and growth trends
- Demographics
- Geographic location of computer
- Psychographics
- Behavior on the Net

Size and Growth Rate

Will the Internet's phenomenal growth rate continue? When television was first introduced, most believed it would grow as a channel of communication. Few predicted that it would be the fastest growing advertising medium in the history of the U.S. Will the Internet continue to grow until it assumes the power of television? Will it remain only one of several media, or will it become one with television and other media? Before investing substantial time and money on maintaining an Internet presence, especially in foreign markets, companies need answers to these questions. There are several ways to measure the Net's size:

- Number of computers connected to the Net
- Sales of products and services directly related to Internet access (e.g., computer modems)
- Number of subscribers to Internet Service Provider firms
- Internet user estimates based on survey research

Demographics

Demographics include such things as age, income and ethnicity. Knowledge of Net audience demographics can aid an organization in determining whether its target markets are online. Where can Net user demographics be found? The U.S. Census Web site provides demographics for the entire population, but not the segment frequenting the Net. Individual Web sites such as Amazon.com collect information from those who complete registration forms. This information is helpful, but far from an all inclusive description of users. It is also proprietary to the company collecting it. The fastest and least expensive source of information about Net user demographics is from research firms and universities that conduct surveys and report results on the Web itself. Several firms provide demographic data, but as the mainstream population adopts the Internet, user composition continues to change rapidly—especially in countries with a low proportion of users. Also, as mentioned in Chapter 3, there are many limitations to primary data that are collected online. There is much controversy over who exactly is "out there."

Geographics

Although the geographic location of computers in cyberspace is not important to users, it is important to companies wanting to be on the Web. The first reason for this is that a company may not wish to distribute its products to the entire planet. If a company only wants to serve France, for example, it will want to know how many Net users are in that location. In fact, there are an increasing number of Web sites that serve only local users. Second, the geographic distribution of users has language implications. Most Net text is currently in the English language, but that is rapidly changing. For example, over 30% of all the discussion in the Usenet is not in English (source: Deja.com), and over 40% of a typical Web site's traffic comes from outside the U.S. (source: www.mediametrix.com). Companies wanting to serve countries that do not speak English may want to create Web pages in other languages. If you visit the Bayer site (the aspirin manufacturer), you will see that the home page offers users a choice of English or German—this practice is becoming increasingly common.

Psychographics

User psychographics include personality, lifestyle, and activities, interests and opinions (AIO). This information can also assist in target market matching, but is especially important for Web page design. For example, if a firm thinks that most Web users are in higher income brackets, it might create pages that appeal to the desire for luxury and success. Web advertisers also want to know about Web users' media habits—do they watch TV, listen to the radio, or read newspapers and magazines? This information will help advertisers decide how to allocate their budgets among various media. There is an increasing amount of psychographic information available on the Web about Net users.

One particularly relevant psychographic variable is a user's attitude towards technology—dubbed by Forrester Research as technographics. According to Forrester, technographics is the single best predictor of Internet adoption.

Behavior

User behavior on the Net is of vital importance to marketers. Companies want to know how much time people spend on the Net, what they do while they are there, how they learn about new Web sites, and what proportion buy merchandise on the Web. It is also important to understand how often users access the Net. Internet adoption is now large enough that we can segment users according to light, medium and heavy usage, by e-mail versus Web use, or by access point: home, school or work.

Finding Answers

Fortunately, much of this information about Net users is available as secondary data. Statistics are reported in traditional media as well as on the Web itself. Businesses can also purchase high quality secondary data from market research firms such as A. C. Nielsen and FIND/SVP. One difficulty is that since these firms sell data, there is a decreasing amount of free information online. In the following exercise, you will do some exploring in order to build a profile of Net user characteristics and behavior using free online secondary data. As you review the statistics you collect, be sure to evaluate their source, how they were collected, and their overall quality and relevance to the research questions.

Planning an E-zine

How big is the Internet, really? This question has no easy answer. For this exercise, you will review several surveys of Internet users to understand the market size and its demographics, geographics, psychographics and Net behavior. You will then use this information to help determine the potential market for an "E-zine," a Web magazine. You will need to determine both the types of articles to include and the kind of products or services that should be advertised based on their appeal to the Web audience.

Why does each survey give a different answer about the size, composition, and behavior of the Net audience? This is a problem inherent in survey research methodology, and is particularly problematic for research conducted online. It is difficult to obtain a random sample of the population and survey participants do not always answer honestly. Because the possibility for error is so great, market researchers tend to be very critical of survey methodology. Much of the information you will review in this exercise has been subject to criticism—but it is the best that we have. The Nielsen TV ratings are always criticized as well, but they are still widely used.

One sticking point is defining who counts as a Net user. For example, if you have a computer in your home that connects to the Internet are you a Net user? What if you've only used it once in the last six months? How about once in the last week? Should we count only regular users? You can begin to see the problem.

CyberAtlas

For this exercise, you will create a magazine with the broadest market appeal. Therefore, you need to develop a profile of the typical Web user. CyberAtlas has done a nice job of compiling research findings from various organizations. They even offer links back to the organizations referenced on their site. Visit CyberAtlas at www.cyberatlas.com. You should see a home page similar to Exhibit 4 - 1. You should be able to answer most questions by using the Stats Toolbox section of the site. If not, try looking at some of the sites referenced at CyberAtlas. One particularly good one is Nua Internet Surveys at www.nua.ie.

Exhibit 4 - 1 CyberAtlas Home Page
Source: cyberatlas.internet.com

Market Size

1. **Users**—Your magazine will be distributed on the Web so you need to know how many folks are "out there." This number is hard to verify, but many firms make estimates. How many people in the world use the Web?

Millions of People	Source	Date

Demographics

2. **Gender**—Is the typical Web user male or female?

Gender	% of users	Source	Date
Male			
Female			

3. **Age**—In order to reach about 50% of Web users, what age ranges would you target? Hint: for this and the following questions you may have to use several categories to build 50% from the survey results.

Age Range	% of users	Source	Date

4. **Education**—In order to reach about 50% of Web users, what education levels would you target?

Education Level	% of users	Source	Date

5. **Income**—What income levels should you target to reach 50% of users?

Income Level	% of users	Source	Date

6. **Occupation**—What occupations would you target to reach 50% of users?

Occupation	% of users	Source	Date

User Behavior

7. **Activities**—What are the top five Internet activities enjoyed by users? This information will help you to design the content and focus for your e-zine.

Activity	% Enjoying	Source

Geographics

8. In the past of few years, the number of users from countries other than North America and Western Europe has grown considerably. Other than North America and Western Europe, what two countries or regions appear to have the best potential for your E-zine?

Country or Region	Statistic as Evidence	Source

Psychographics—Stanford Research Institute (SRI) VALS

Many marketers who wish to understand the psychographics of both existing and potential customers use SRI's Values and Lifestyles Program (VALS). SRI categorizes people by two dimensions: self-identity and resources. The philosophy is that consumers purchase products that shape their identities using psychological, physical, demographic and material resources. SRI developed a series of questionnaires to measure these attributes and then placed respondents in lifestyle groups. Note that the VALS server is occasionally down on weekends, so if you can't get through just try again in a day or two. Also, if the VALS survey is not on there, go ahead and take any of the VALS surveys that are online (e.g. VALS2, iVALS) and use your results to answer the questions.

9. Visit SRI at future.sri.com and follow links to the VALS questionnaire. Take the survey and list your type here.

10. Briefly describe the activities of your VALS type.

11. According to SRI, Actualizers are more than 30% of the Web population. Briefly describe the kinds of activities this segment enjoys. This will help you design your e-zine.

Putting It All Together

12. Describe a typical Web user (demographic profile).

13. Based on what you learned about Internet users, what content area and appeal would you choose for your magazine?

14. Produce a title for your magazine.

15. Write titles for two articles you'd include in your new magazine based on this information.

16. What products and services might advertise in your magazine?

Leveraging Technology

Audience Measurement Challenge

Measuring Web site traffic has become a big business precisely because it is difficult to do well. Advertisers demand accurate and verifiable measures before they will pay for ads on sites. Rarely are they willing to accept the claims of the sites themselves—rather the advertisers seek out the services of third party measurement firms. These third party services will audit the log file of the Web site. They take a sample from the log file and then generate usage statistics. The process is similar to auditing the subscription list for a magazine. However, the measurement companies have known for some time that the readership is always greater than the subscription list. Why? Because multiple readers view each issue. For example, many people read magazines in doctors' offices and health clubs. As a result magazine companies conduct readership surveys to estimate this "pass along" readership. The Web has a similar problem. Many organizations actually make copies of Web sites and then let their employees access the copies. This is done to speed access since a local copy will load far faster than one pulled off of the Internet. The process is accomplished by use of a proxy server, which keeps the copy at the corporate site. The problem however is that the original site now has no record of visits to the proxy server. And unfortunately for Web sites there are no agreed upon standards for audience multipliers—though some studies indicate that as much as 70% of the readership is not counted. Consequently, one measurement company, MatchLogic, discovered how to count this readership in a clever way. While it allows the Web site to be copied or cached by proxy servers, it does not allow the ads to be similarly cached. In fact it doesn't store ads permanently on the Web page. Instead it programs the Web page itself to request a new ad from MatchLogic's ad server every time that it is viewed. The ad server counts the requests and the measurement problem is solved. See Exhibit 4 - 2.

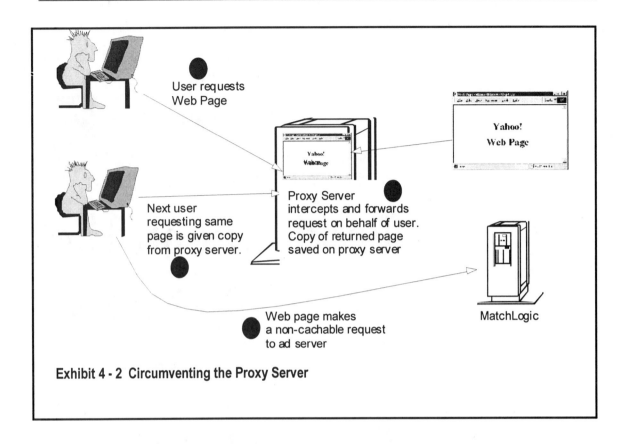

Exhibit 4 - 2 Circumventing the Proxy Server

Chapter 5

Products on the Internet

Estimated time: 110 minutes

Chapter Outline

- Online Product Opportunities
  - New Product Opportunities
  - Product Mix Strategies
  - Branding and Trademarks
- New Products in the Media Industry
  - Media Categorized by Media Type
  - Media Characterized by Product Design Strategy
  - How Do Media Firms Make Money?
- Comparing Traditional and Online Media
  - Newspaper - New York Times
  - Magazine
  - Television
  - Putting It All Together
- Leveraging Technology
  - Multimedia

Learning Objectives

- Identify new product opportunities based on Internet technology
- Apply product mix strategies to online media firms
- Understand the importance of online branding
- Explain the problems for broadcast media using the online channel
- Explore online versions of print and broadcast media
- Explain the role of advertising and subscriptions for online media

Online Product Opportunities

Prior to this chapter, we presented the Net as a tool for marketing planning. Marketers use the Net for primary and secondary research, which aids in decision making. In this chapter, we introduce the Net as *part* of the marketing mix. A product is something that satisfies the needs of organizations or consumers and for which they are willing to exchange money or other items of value. Products can be tangible items, intangible services, people, ideas, places, or any combination of these things. The Internet is useful for product planning: it is a resource for gathering information about competitors, patents, consumers, and other environmental issues. In addition, Internet technology has spawned a vast number of new products. New firms and brands, such as Amazon, emerged to capitalize on Internet opportunities. Existing firms have also created new Internet products, modified existing products for online distribution, or offered current products for sale through their Web sites. Some new products such as search engines are unique to the Internet while other products such as CD's simply use the Internet as a new distribution channel. In this chapter we consider only new products or product adaptations: existing products that are sold online are discussed in the distribution chapter. Three important concerns for product planners are new product opportunities, product mix strategies, and branding decisions.

New Product Opportunities

Examples of truly innovative products are Web portals such as Yahoo!, software to develop Web pages, services that audit the traffic at Web sites, and a whole list of new technologies such as cable modems. New product opportunities exist in three main areas:

- **Hardware**—This includes modems, PC's, Web servers, and switching and routing equipment to send data between users and content providers.

- **Software**—Web authoring programs, Web browsers, security encryption software, and search robots are examples in this area.

- **Services**—Some of the innovations made possible by the Internet include Web site development agencies, page designers, ISP's, shopping agents, and search engines.

Product Mix Strategies

Taking a less risky step, some companies use the Internet to extend their current brands: examples include online stock brokerage services and newspaper publishing. Three important product mix strategies exist for firms considering offering products on the Internet. Firms will use one or more for various product mix additions.

- **Discontinuous innovations**—These are new-to-the-world products never seen before, such as a Web search engine. These products will carry a new brand name. This is a very risky strategy with a big payoff for success.

- **New product lines**—When a firm takes an existing brand and uses it for products in a different category it is employing this strategy. Microsoft introduced a new line with its Internet Explorer.

- **Additions to existing lines**—This occurs when a firm adds a new product to a current line, such as the New York Times did when it when it created a special version of the daily newspaper for the Internet. This strategy is the least risky of all three.

Branding and Trademarks

A brand is a name, (McDonald's), a symbol (golden arches), or other identifying information. When a firm registers that information with the U.S. Patent office, it becomes a trademark, and thus is legally protected from imitation. Organizations spend a lot of time and money developing strong, unique brand names. Using the company trademark in the Web address helps consumers quickly find the site. For example, www.coca-cola.com adds power to Coca-Cola brands. The problem is that many companies in the world share the same names, but they cannot all have the same Web address (e.g., Delta Airlines and Delta Faucet). This is a problem many people are trying to solve as the Internet grows. For more information see www.networksolutions.com, one of the firms that assigns Web site addresses.

In addition to the site address, it is important for firms to decide whether Internet products will carry existing brand names, or whether they will create new brand names for Internet products. For example, the folks at *Wired* magazine created *HotWired* for their Internet "E-Zine," while *Time* magazine applied the brand name in both places.

New Products in the Media Industry

Development of digital media content and programs is a revolutionary practice made possible by the Internet. Suppliers can deliver content directly to the consumer on demand without using the U.S. Postal Service or the network of delivery trucks and carriers that brings newspapers and magazines to your door. Media firms are currently experimenting with various product strategies for Internet distribution. Should these firms introduce discontinuous innovations, new lines, or simply add to existing lines? Should they create new brands or use current brands for online versions? This exercise asks you to investigate several products of media firms to identify their product strategies. First, a few definitions will be helpful. Internet media are categorized by type (print, broadcast) and by product design strategy (degree of similarity to traditional product).

Media Categorized by Media Type

Traditional media are categorized by print (newspapers, magazines) and broadcast (radio, television). This discrimination is muddied when media firms distribute over the Internet because the technology allows all media firms to send content in any format from lowly text to full multimedia (e.g., online newspapers may include audio and video clips). Also, the computer receives radio and television programs, so should the medium still be called "radio" or "television?" For this exercise, however, we'll stick with the traditional definitions because they accurately describe media firms at this time.

- **Print media**—Traditional print media were among the first companies to go online in 1994. It was relatively easy for magazines and newspapers to convert articles and pictures into Web pages. Print media require relatively little bandwidth. Text loads very quickly on an online publication, though pictures take a bit more time to load.

- **Broadcast media**

  - **Radio**—Audio media include radio broadcasts of both talk and music. As the Internet's bandwidth increased and modems became faster, radio stations began to broadcast live audio transmissions at their Web sites. Unlike print media, however, radio stations must purchase special software to distribute "product" to online listeners. Also, because of low bandwidth, audio does not always come across the Net smoothly. For these and other reasons, some radio stations still don't broadcast over the Internet. Users can download free Real Player software to listen to online radio, and RealAudio boasts over 38 million users: this is a high growth area online. The exercise in this chapter doesn't include radio, so you might want to visit the British Broadcasting Corporation (www.bbc.co.uk) and explore one of its radio stations or check out your local station at www.broadcast.com.

  - **Television**—If radio is lagging, television is even farther behind. The problem is not the computer receivers: Windows 98 and 2000 users can view television programs right on the desktop. The biggest barrier for TV stations is the Internet's low bandwidth: video takes up a lot of space and cannot yet be delivered smoothly over the Net. Consequently, one usually sees video clips in RealPlayer or QuickTime format rather than live broadcasts.

Is it only a matter of time before all media create products for the Internet? We think the answer is yes and here is why—bandwidth is increasing. Most importantly, the last leg of the Internet—the connection to the home—now has three high-speed options. Home users can purchase cable modems from their cable company, DSL modems from their phone company, or a satellite dish from DirecPC. However, cable modems and DSL are available primarily in affluent areas. Nonetheless, market penetration is increasing—especially for cable modems.

Media Characterized by Product Design Strategy

- **Identical content**—Some media companies such as Internet World place identical content on the Internet and in their paper publications. In this case, the Internet is simply a new distribution channel.

- **Overlapping content**—Some media companies such as the New York Times produce an online version which incorporates some of the traditional content along with Internet only features which appeal to the online audience. The online version is an addition to the existing product line.

- **Complementary content**—Some media companies use their Internet channel to complement, extend, or cross-sell their traditional channel. For example, NBC uses its Internet channel, MSNBC, to provide more in depth coverage of stories that originate on the traditional network. NBC applied a new brand name to its Internet product that might be considered a discontinuous innovation—never before did consumers have a chance to chat with people in the news stories!

How Do Media Firms Make Money?

Some online media firms charge no money for their content but make money selling ads. Others charge for content either via subscriptions or *a la carte*. Still others use a mixed model charging no fees for current content but charging a small fee *a la carte* for archived content.

- **Subscriptions**—For newspapers and magazines, subscription fees are a very small proportion of the firm's revenues—oftentimes they don't even cover the cost of delivering the publication. Publishers and broadcasters are trying to use the subscription model in cyberspace; however, they are not too successful yet. Most Internet users will not pay a fee to view Web pages, including those of newspapers and magazines. One exception is the Wall Street Journal that is successfully charging a monthly fee for subscribers.

- **Ad supported**—There are no subscription fees for traditional broadcast media because they are entirely advertiser supported. Even though one pays a fee for cable TV, that money goes to the cable company and not to the stations. This means that advertisers must generate profits for these firms, and although Internet advertising revenues are increasing, most media firms are not yet making a profit on their Web sites. So why are they doing it? To build audience market share for the future when advertising online becomes widely accepted by advertisers. Another reason media firms maintain Web sites is to cross promote their traditional media offerings.

The Internet is only one distribution channel for media firms. Most media offer both traditional publications/broadcasts and online versions. Which stories should be run online and which in the daily newspaper? How many stories should be included in the online version as opposed to the traditional version? These are product decisions plaguing each media firm during the Internet's infancy. In this exercise we'll ask you to review several online media offerings and ask you to compare them to the traditional forms, making conclusions about your findings. Important comparison criteria include:

- **Content**—The words, graphics, audio and video that were created by the media firm to appear as the stories or programming on the site. Do they appear to be identical or different (overlapping, complementary) from the traditional version?

- **Format**—The overall look of the Web site. Does the online newspaper, radio broadcast, or other medium look and sound like its traditional counterpart?

- **Geographic distribution**—Does the online medium appear to be distributed to different geographic areas than the traditional version? To evaluate this, consider Internet users versus traditional audiences, and also check for existence of foreign language translations in the online version.

- **Advertising**—How much advertising is online versus what you might see in the traditional version of each medium? You might answer this in terms of proportion of space dedicated to ads. Do the types of advertisers differ?

- **Subscription fees**—Does the online version charge any fees for accessing content? Does this differ from the traditional version?

- **Unusual services**—Many online media provide services that are not available in traditional counterparts. Some examples include weather databases, search functions, product sales, and the ability to personalize the Web page based on interests.

The New York Times
ON THE WEB

NYC
Weather
32° F

SATURDAY, FEBRUARY 19, 2000 | Site Updated 1:40 AM

QUICK NEWS
PAGE ONE PLUS
International
National/N.Y.
Politics
Business
Technology
Science/Health
Sports
Weather
Opinion
Arts
Automobiles
Books
CareerPath
Diversions
Living
Magazine

Large Turnout Is Anticipated For South Carolina's Primary

By RICHARD L. BERKE
FROM SATURDAY'S TIMES
The fierce struggle between Gov. George W. Bush and Senator John McCain has stirred such keen interest that strategists on both sides predicted that turnout would far exceed the state's presidential primary record. Go to Article
•South Carolina Finds Bush Snug in Father's Suit

(NYT)
Some Native Americans want this 15-ton meteorite returned to Oregon, not displayed in the Museum of Natural History's new planetarium. Go to Article

Exhibit 5 - 1 NY Times on the Web
Source: www.nyt.com ©2000 The New York Times Company. Reprinted by Permission

Comparing Traditional and Online Media

Newspaper - New York Times

Note: before you start this exercise you might want to review question 7: Putting it all together.

1. Visit www.nytimes.com, register, then complete the following table and answer the question. Even if you haven't read the NY Times, you can answer based on your knowledge of newspapers in general. We suggest taking the guided quick tour of the NY Times Web site and visiting the help center.

Comparison criterion	Differences from a typical traditional newspaper
Content	
Format	
Geographic distribution	
Advertising	
Subscription fees	
Unusual services	

2. Describe anything you see on the site that suggests you subscribe to the traditional newspaper (cross promotion).

Magazine

3. Using a search tool, find the online version of your favorite magazine. Review the Web site and complete the table.

Name of magazine _____

Comparison criterion	Differences from the printed version of your magazine
Content	
Format	
Geographic distribution	
Advertising	

Comparison criterion	Differences from the printed version of your magazine
Subscription fees	
Unusual services	

4. Describe anything you see on the site that suggests you subscribe to the traditional magazine.

Television

5. Visit MSNBC at www.msnbc.com. Check out the site and compare it to NBC's traditional television broadcasting. Complete the following table.

Comparison criterion	Differences from traditional television
Content	
Format	
Geographic distribution	
Advertising	
Subscription fees	
Unusual services	

6. Describe anything you see on the site that suggests you watch NBC on the television.

Putting It All Together

7. Now reflect on what you have learned so far to complete the following chart. For each medium you explored, make a conjecture about what strategy was used and complete the table.

   - **Product mix strategy**: discontinuous innovation, new product line, addition to existing product line

   - **Branding strategy**: traditional/online brand names the same or different?

   - **Product design strategy**: identical content, overlapping content, complementary content

	NY Times Newspaper	Magazine	MSNBC Television
Product mix strategy			
Branding strategy			
Product design strategy			

8. In general, what differences and similarities did you find between online and offline versions of these three media types?

   Differences:

   Similarities:

Leveraging Technology

Multimedia

One of the hottest trends and greatest challenges for content providers is the delivery of multimedia content over the Web. It's a challenge because most home connections to the Web are slow (low bandwidth) and multimedia requires high bandwidth. There are four solutions to the problem:

1. Speed up the home Internet connection using either a cable modem from the cable company or a DSL modem from the phone company. Both cable modems and DSL provide high bandwidth connections capable of carrying multimedia. One reason AOL purchased Time Warner was to use the latter company's cable division to distribute high bandwidth content via cable modems.

2. Compress the multimedia content into smaller packets of information. RealNetworks has been the pioneer in the compression of multimedia. They began with compression of audio (RealAudio) and moved to compression of video (RealVideo). The compression is so good that it operates over a low bandwidth connection, albeit with rather choppy delivery. Another popular compression technology for music is MP3 which can reduce CD recordings to one tenth their original size.

3. Stream the multimedia so that the user can play a piece of it while the rest downloads. The alternative would of course be to wait for the entire audio or video clip to download before you could listen to any of it.

4. Distribute multiple copies of the multimedia content around the Internet so that it is closer to the end users. By distributing content, delays which might be caused by the Internet itself are avoided.

Combinations of all of the above techniques may be employed to speed content delivery over the Internet. However, the most important is to speed up the Internet connection to the home using cable modems or DSL. Currently, about 2 million households have high speed connections with the number expected to grow to 25 million by 2004 (www.strategis.com). Already the installed base is large enough to support Web sites that cater to multimedia content.

Chapter **6**

Price Planning on the Net

Estimated time: 120 minutes

Learning Objectives

- Understand the role of price in commodity service markets
- Discuss the factors putting upward and downward pressure on Internet pricing
- Identify several pricing strategies
- Demonstrate an understanding of how pricing strategy varies with demand
- Describe the relationship of pricing to other consumer decision variables

Online Pricing Pressures

Online pricing strategies parallel offline strategies. That is, firms set overall strategies based on their marketing objectives and then fine-tune for individual products and markets. Many internal and external factors influence prices: marketing objectives, costs, product demand, competitive environment, and government influences. Businesses are still experimenting with pricing strategies on the Internet, but one thing is true about Internet pricing: There is tremendous downward pressure. Another emerging truth is that an increasing amount of price negotiation occurs online: more so than offline. Some examples include online auctions and many sites that encourage price bidding such as www.priceline.com. This section describes factors putting downward pressure on pricing, suggests several areas of cost increases on the Internet channel, and concludes with three low price strategies appropriate for the current pricing environment.

Factors Putting Downward Pressure on Internet Prices

There are many forces driving prices down in the Internet channel. These include the following:

1. **Shopping agents**—Consumers can easily search nationwide or even worldwide for the lowest price on a given item. Shopping agents such as PriceSCAN (www.pricescan.com) facilitate these searches by displaying the results in a comparative format. Since the results are listed in order with the lowest price first, outlets that are not price competitive risk being left off of the first screen and might as well be invisible.

2. **Tax free zones**—Since most online retailing takes place across state lines, there are often no taxes to pay on purchases. Eliminating the 5% to 8% sales tax reduces the consumer's out of pocket expenditure. Although states and foreign governments have challenged the Internet tax-free zone, the U.S. Government continues to support a moratorium on taxes for Internet purchases.

3. **Venture capital**—Many Internet companies are financed through venture capital or angel investors. Many investors take a long-term view with Internet companies and are willing to sustain losses in the short term in order to let those companies grow. They understand that the most important goal is to establish brand equity and grab market share. Companies operating under this halo are willing to sustain losses for up to five years in order to promote their brand. Therefore, they can sell below fair market value since they do not operate under a profit maximization pricing objective.

4. **Lower costs**—Costs are often lower in this channel, and that can result in either higher profits or lower prices. Because of the reasons just identified, the current effect is to put downward pressure on Internet pricing. Following are some of the online cost savings:

    a. **Order processing**—Since customers fill out their own order forms, firms save the expense of order entry personnel and paper processing. These expenses can be considerable. The cost of producing and processing an invoice electronically is $10 on average, compared with $100 in offline transactions, and an average retail banking transaction costs $0.15 to $0.20 online versus $1.50 offline.[1] Cisco Systems, the world's largest manufacturer of networking equipment, allows Web-based orders from its customers. The paperwork reduction it reaps from this saves hundreds of millions of dollars each year.

b. **Inventory**—Some firms do not even hold inventory, saving considerably on financing costs. Rather they acquire the inventory in response to the customer's order or have it drop-shipped from a business partner.

c. **Overhead**—Online storefronts are able to lower their overhead costs since they do not have to rent and staff expensive retail space. Amazon's warehouses are considerably less expensive to rent and staff than the retail space of a trendy shopping mall. Furthermore, these warehouses can be located in areas with low rents, low wages, low taxes, and quick access to shipping hubs.

d. **Customer service**—Customer service requests average $15 to $20 in an offline call center versus $3 to $5 when customers help themselves on the Internet.[1]

e. **Printing and mailing**—Firms do not incur mail distribution and printing costs for their product catalogs. Once the catalog is placed online, there is little or no incremental cost for access. The same holds true for e-mail promotions.

Costs Putting Upward Pressure on Internet Prices

There are also factors that increase the costs of products sold online. Unless marketers can raise prices, these narrow the gap between costs and prices and lower profits.

1. **Distribution**—Online retailers face hefty distribution costs for their products since each product must be shipped separately to its destination. This is similar to the catalog marketer's cost structure. Most retailers pass on this shipping cost to their customers and reveal it only at the conclusion of the order entry process. Hiding exorbitant shipping and handling costs until the last minute offends many customers. In some cases the shipping cost cancels out the cost savings.

2. **Affiliate programs**—Many Web sites pay a commission on referrals through a affiliate programs. These programs reward the referring Web site by paying a 7% to 15% commission on the sale. This commission, like all channel intermediary costs, has the effect of inflating the price of the item or lowering company profits.

3. **Site development and maintenance**—Web site development and maintenance is not cheap. Forrester research estimates the cost for a "conservative" site to be $10,000 to $100,000, while an "aggressive" site costs $1 million or more—and that is just to develop the site. Maintenance can be quite expensive, especially with hardware, software, and monthly Internet connection costs.

4. **Marketing and advertising**—Online marketing and advertising costs tend to be higher than their offline equivalents. A survey by the Boston Consulting Group found that 43% of online revenue goes to marketing and advertising whereas only 14.2% of revenue covers the same costs for offline department stores.[2]

Downward price pressure paints a gloomy picture for marketers, unless costs are low enough to allow a decent profit. In balance, many factors such as lower distribution and communication costs ease the situation substantially, but the fact remains that few firms are profitable online. In the end, a marketer must create digital value for users and do it better than the competition in order to draw advertisers and sell product at profitable prices.

Online Pricing Strategies

There are a variety of possible online pricing strategies. These include:

- **Penetration pricing**—Penetration pricing is the practice of charging a low price for a product for the purpose of gaining market share. This strategy is particularly effective in a price-sensitive market like the Internet. America Online adopted this strategy when it adopted the $19.95 monthly flat rate Internet access a couple years ago. An AOL spokesperson explained that the firm was trying to buy "real estate." AOL wanted every desktop it could get, even at a financial loss, so that it could deliver users to marketers. The strategy worked: Today AOL is the largest Internet hub, with 54 million unique visitors each month (www.mediametrix.com). Lots of money is pouring in as AOL makes deals with others who want access to those desktops.

- **Price leadership**—A price leader is the lowest-priced product entry in a particular category. In the offline world, Wal-Mart is a price leader, setting the pace for other retailers. With shopping agents on the Web, a price leader strategy is sweet indeed. In order to implement this strategy, however, marketers must shave costs to a minimum. This can be done through Internet marketing cost efficiencies described earlier, but a firm must do it better than the competition. Often the largest producer is able to be the price leader because of economies of scale, but on the Internet an entrepreneur operating out of a basement constantly challenges the large producer. This is a productive strategy on the Internet, but competition is fierce and price leadership is often fleeting. Of course, the second-lowest-priced item will also gain sales, especially if it offers advantages over the price leader's product entry.

- **Promotional pricing**—Many online retailers have turned to promotional pricing to encourage a first purchase, to encourage repeat business, and to close a sale. In many cases the promotion has an expiration date which helps to close the sale. Promotional pricing on the Internet has at least three advantages. First, it can be highly targeted through e-mail messages. Second, research shows high customer satisfaction with Internet purchases. Doing everything possible to attract a customer is good business. Third, research shows that customers are more loyal online than offline. Customers would much prefer to remain loyal to an Internet store that has given them good service than to risk their credit information and bad service somewhere else.

- **Market skimming pricing**—Market skimming pricing introduces products at a high price which will only attract the early adopters. The company then steadily drops the price as it introduces newer high end models. At each lower price point the product attracts a new group of customers as it continues through the product life cycle.

- **Product line pricing**—Many manufacturers offer product lines which range in price from inexpensive to expensive models. For example, Toyota may sell a consumer a low priced Echo while she is in college with the expectation that she will upgrade to a Camry upon graduation. Product line pricing attempts to capture multiple market segments while building brand loyalty.

Elasticity of Demand

Airline tickets are a price-driven market for most customers. Many will trade off non-stop flights, preferred travel times, and choice of airline to get the lowest possible price. Therefore, airlines offer advance purchase discounts to make sure they fill as many seats as possible. Demand tends to be very elastic, as evidenced by the heavy reservation activity that takes place during fare wars. Notable exceptions include first class travelers and business travelers. First class travelers are easily segmented–they get a better seat; but business travelers often sit in coach. Ever wonder why you get a cheaper fare when you have a Saturday night stay? It's because the business traveler is willing to pay a premium to fly out and return home in the same workweek. Vacation travelers by contrast are willing to spend Saturday night. In this exercise we are going to plan a flight online in order to observe the price elasticity in this industry.

Expedia is a comprehensive travel site developed by Microsoft and then spun off as a separate company. The site allows consumers to book flights, reserve hotel rooms and rent cars online. Sign onto the Expedia Web site at www.expedia.com. Register a new account; it's free. Then price a round-trip flight from New York (any airport) to Paris (any airport) traveling coach class, departing tomorrow, and returning one day after you arrive. Record Expedia's response in the table below. Then press the Search Again button and vary the criteria to complete the rest of the table:

Class	Departing	Returning After	Airline & Departure Flight	Price
Coach	Tomorrow	1 day		
Coach	Tomorrow	1 week		
Coach	Next Month	1 day		
Coach	Next Month	1 week		
First	Tomorrow	1 day		
First	Tomorrow	1 week		
First	Next Month	1 day		
First	Next Month	1 week		

1.   What can you conclude from this example about the elasticity of demand for coach fares? For first-class fares?

2.   Do you think the higher price for a first class seat is justified by higher costs to the airline?

3. How do the prices differ for one day versus one week trips? How can you explain this?

4. For first class, do the prices differ for trips departing tomorrow versus next month? Why or why not?

5. J.D. Power and Associates is a marketing information firm. They conduct surveys of customer satisfaction in different industries. Visit their Web site at www.jdpower.com and record which airline ranks highest in customer satisfaction. As a consumer would this influence your choice in airline? How much more (if any) are you willing to pay for travel satisfaction?

Don't buy it without a PriceSCAN!

At PriceSCAN, we want to save you money and help take the hassle out of shopping. Check out our **unbiased** price and product information and see how.

All shopping guides are not created equal. To find out why click here.

_____

Ready to start shopping?
Begin by clicking on one of the categories below:

Books

Computers
Hardware, Software, Supplies, WebTV

Office Equipment
Calculators, Copiers, Label Makers, Fax Machines, Shredders, Typewriters

Sponsored By

Pick Store ▾

Exhibit 6 - 1 PriceSCAN Shopping Agent
Source: www.pricescan.com

Shopping Agents

Expedia's ability to find the lowest price fare available anywhere in the world is a model being adapted to the retail industry as well. Shopping agents, which can scan the Internet in search of the lowest prices, are beginning to emerge. Some of the better known agents may be found at Shopper.com (www.shopper.com), mySimon (www.mysimon.com), PriceSCAN (www.pricescan.com), and iTrack (www.itrack.com). Some agents specialize in product categories whereas others seek to be comprehensive. Some agents report on all firms selling particular products, while others only search a few of the firms. The agents have the obvious effect of putting a downward pressure on prices since the consumer will tend to choose the cheapest supplier, all other things being equal. There is also a psychological effect created by the shopping agent since consumers may surmise that if the agent recommends the site, the site is probably reputable—otherwise why would they jeopardize their own reputation by continuing to list it? Most of the agents support one click transfers to the desired retailer.

6. Visit the PriceSCAN shopping agent at www.pricescan.com and conduct a search for a PC compatible notebook computer system. Find a system whose speed is at least 450 MHz and has at least a 15 inch display (do not specify a preference for other features). Complete the following table for a mid-price notebook meeting these criteria—use current prices. (Hint: click on the notebook to reveal all the vendors who carry that notebook and the link to the price trend graph).

Manufacturer	Model	High Price	Low Price	Average Price

7. Is the average price for the notebook increasing or decreasing? How would you explain this?

8. Are the high/low/average prices converging or diverging over time? How would you explain this?

9. What pricing strategy do you think appropriate to market this notebook? Why? (hint: Locate and visit the Web sites of vendors that market the notebook and list any evidence you find to support your pricing strategy.)

10. Based on your observation of the price trend for this notebook where would you place it on the product life cycle and why? (Hint: if the high/low/average prices converge over time then the product is nearing the end of its life cycle.)

Leveraging Technology

How Shopping Agents Work

In the leveraging technology section of chapter 1, we learned that search engines do their searching weeks in advance and store the information in a database that users query. Shopping agents do not have this luxury. Buyers expect that the price listed by the shopping agent is accurate as of that day. Therefore the shopping agent's database must be updated daily. The database must at a minimum include category, manufacturer, model, vendors and prices for each item listed. For high involvement products, benefit information (e.g., CPU speed and screen size) is usually stored as well.

The clever folks at PriceSCAN found that they were able to mine this data longitudinally over time for the consumer's benefit. This is how they produce the price trend graphs that we saw in the chapter exercise. Consider for a moment that this information would be virtually impossible to compile on your own.

Obviously gathering the data represents a lot of work. Fortunately much of the work can be automated. Typically a shopping agent will have a fixed set of vendors from which it retrieves pricing information. Shopping agents such as mySimon are taught how to navigate each merchant's Web site and extract pricing information in an automated fashion. Some agents such as PriceSCAN include information from magazine ads and product catalogs as well. This additional information must be entered by hand.

To speed shopping some agents use a technique called parallel pull. Requests for pricing information are sent out simultaneously (in parallel) to all relevant vendors in the agent's database. As the prices come back they are organized in a table which is presented to the user.

For whom is the agent really working? Some agents such as PriceSCAN pride themselves on representing only the buyer's interests. They do not charge vendors a fee for listing. Other agents may charge a fee for listing and additional fees for preferred placement in the listings. This model is similar to the yellow pages which allow vendors to place ads early in the listings. Unlike the yellow pages, however, the consumer has access to pricing information and is usually able to sort the listings by price even if the initial list is ordered by preferred placement.

[1]Mougayar, Walid (1997), *Opening Digital Markets*. New York: McGraw-Hill.

[2]Machlis, Sharon (1998), "Warning: Web Selling Isn't Cheap," *Computerworld* (October 12: Vol. 32, No. 41).

Chapter **7**

The Net as Distribution Channel

Estimated time: 90 minutes

Chapter Outline

- Online Distribution Channels
- Direct Channel: Digital Products
- Indirect Channel: Online Auctions
    Auctions classified by market
    Auctions classified by type of auction
    Additional Services
    How do Auction Houses Make Money?
- Online Retailing: "e-tailing"
- Leveraging Technology
    Site Rating Services

Learning Objectives

- Understand the Net as a direct distribution channel for digital products
- Describe the current status of music delivered over the Net
- Discuss the Net as an indirect distribution channel
- Give an example of an online retailer and an agent intermediary
- Identify several types of auctions
- Describe several services offered by online auction houses
- Explain the Net as electronic retailer in the distribution channel

Online Distribution Channels

The Internet is an important new distribution channel (the "place" component of the four P's). In this chapter we'll review the distribution function, then explore three major developments.

A distribution channel is a set of firms and individuals that facilitate the movement of product from producer to business user or consumer. Many companies use marketing intermediaries, such as wholesalers and retailers, between them and the consumer. These intermediaries often take ownership of the product and resell it to other intermediaries along the channel. This type of channel is called an **indirect** distribution channel. A typical indirect channel includes a manufacturer, wholesaler, retailer, and consumer. If no intermediaries are used, the channel is **direct**: product flows directly from producer to consumer or business user.

The Internet created reallocation of distribution channel functions, oftentimes to unlikely firms. In traditional automobile channels, for example, car dealers sold product, provided financing, and offered repair services. On the Net, new metamediaries do all this and more for a number of automobile companies on one Web site. In particular, the Net spawned three trends in distribution--disintermediation (e.g., selling software directly to consumers), new intermediaries (e.g., shopping agents bringing buyers and sellers together online), and metamediation (e.g., providing information and referrals for all aspects of a wedding, including reception sites, flowers, the cake, dresses, and the wedding registry).[1] Disintermediation results in lower costs to consumers and/or higher margins for the manufacturer. New intermediaries drive costs back up because there are more firms profiting from the sale. The metamediaries are particularly interesting since they are often organized around major purchases such as automobiles (www.Edmunds.com) or major life events such as weddings (www.theknot.com). Metamediaries save consumers enormous amounts of time by grouping related services on a single site and providing trusted information content. For example, Edmunds provides auto reviews, links to auto suppliers, insurers, financers, warranties, and after market options.

The Distribution channel is one marketing function most affected by the Internet. There are a number of exciting developments. This chapter will explore three of those developments:

- **Direct Channel: Digital Products**—Direct distribution of media, music and software.

- **Indirect Channel: Online Auctions**—Buying and selling on online auctions.

- **Online Retailing**—Buying and selling on online storefronts. This can be done either directly from manufacturer to consumer or indirectly through one or more intermediaries.

Direct Channel: Digital Products

Direct distribution of media content, music, and software is a revolutionary practice made possible by the Internet. Suppliers can deliver content directly to the consumer on demand without using the U.S. Postal Service or the network of delivery trucks and carriers that typically deliver products to your door. In fact, any digital product can be delivered directly over the Net.

- **Media**—Magazine and newspaper publishers create text and graphics and put them on Web sites for your review. Most are advertising supported, however some charge a subscription. Radio stations broadcast live using digital audio, and television stations are beginning to send video over the Net.

- **Music**—Many online music stores such as CDNow allow customers to sample 30 seconds of a CD track prior to making a purchase. As of this writing, the major record companies were not allowing the entire content of a CD to be transferred over the Internet. Their concern—piracy. In addition to this, CD tracks are enormous files around 50MB in size. However, a compression scheme called MP3 allows CD tracks to shrink to about 1/10th of their size. This allows individual tracks or even an entire CD to be downloaded over the Internet. The music can be played back on the user's computer or via a portable Walkman™ like device called the Rio. True to the music industry's fears, bootleg copies of CDs have appeared on the Internet. Lycos and Real.com even have search engines that help you locate MP3 files online. Napster.com provides software to turn any user's computer into a music server whose available titles will be cataloged on the Napster site for the Internet community. Napster has been so popular on college campuses that many universities now block access to Napster.

- **Software**—One can purchase or sample software online: the supplier allows users to download directly over the Net to a computer.

Indirect Channel: Online Auctions

Online auctions are exploding in popularity on the Internet. You can find auctions on almost any item. Once the province of online auction houses such as Onsale and eBay, auctions are now offered by retailers such as Sharper Image and Amazon.com. In addition to selling products through traditional and online retail stores, these firms serve as intermediary agents when they bring buyers and sellers together in auctions. Auctions may be classified according to the markets (consumer or business) and according to the type of auction (Yankee, Dutch, and so forth.). Most auction houses offer a number of additional services such as escrow accounts and community forums.

Auctions classified by market

- **Business to Business** auctions are generally not available to the public—even for viewing. Such auctions often involve thousands or millions of dollars for big ticket items such as natural gas purchases. They are becoming increasingly popular with businesses in commodity markets such as metals or in any businesses seeking to unload surplus inventory.

- **Business to Consumer** auctions allow established retailers or wholesalers to sell excess inventory or odd lot sizes. Some of these retailers offer their own auctions as a part of their Web site. For example, Egghead.com, an online retailer of computer products, runs Surplusauction.com. Similarly, Sharper Image runs an auction on their site. Other retailers use an established auction house such as Onsale to sell their inventory.

- **Consumer to Consumer** auctions provide a forum for individuals to sell to other individuals. The largest of these auction houses, eBay, lists over 3.5 million items in nearly 2,900 categories. On a daily basis eBay attracts more traffic than Amazon.com though many of these are return visitors checking up on their auctions. (source: www.mediametrix.com). Some individuals, so called powersellers, sell high enough volumes to make a living at eBay.

Auctions classified by type of auction

- **Regular auction**—Regular auctions are also called basic or standard auctions. This is the type of auction with which you may be most familiar. The seller specifies a start price, stop time, and a minimum increment for bids. The sale goes to the highest bidder.

- **Reserve auction**—A variation on the regular auction in which the seller establishes a minimum price below which she will not sell the item. The reserve price is not revealed to the bidders though the public is notified as soon as bidding exceeds the reserve price.

- **Automatic bidding**—Automatic bidding is not really a type of auction but rather an option you may use with regular or reserve auctions. With automatic bidding you secretly set the maximum price you are willing to bid. A software agent then goes to work for you increasing your bid in response to other bidders' agents. If the current bid exceeds your maximum, then your agent stops bidding. Otherwise, your agent tries to win the bid.

- **Dutch auction**—The seller offers multiple items for sale. The top bidders all receive the item at the very same price—the lowest winning bid. Imagine that the seller has two copies of a Ricky Martin CD. The high bid on the CD's is $11; the second highest bid is $9. Both of the high bidders get the CD for $9— the lowest winning bid.

- **Yankee auction**—A variation on the Dutch auction where the high bidders pay different prices. For the example cited above the high bidder would pay $11 for the CD whereas the second highest bidder would pay only $9. This is one time in life when it pays to be the runner up!

- **Reverse auction**—The hottest trend in Internet auctions is reverse auctions. In a reverse auction the user specifies the price she is willing to pay for a product or service such as an airline ticket. Suppliers bid for the user's business by trying to get closer to the user's price than any other supplier and thus win the user's business.

Additional Services

- **Reputation services**—As odd as it may seem auction houses are one of the few places in cyberspace (or elsewhere) that your reputation follows you in a highly documented form. At the conclusion of a sale, the buyer and seller have an opportunity to rate one another both numerically and with written comments. These comments are stored by the auction house and are publicly accessible. The function of the ratings is to help buyer and seller evaluate one another's reputability. After all, money will be changing hands. The buyer wants to be sure that if she sends a check, the seller will deliver the goods. The seller wants to be sure that the buyer pays on time and does not bounce checks.

- **Insurance**—Some auction houses offer free insurance up to a couple of hundred dollars to protect buyers and sellers through a transaction.

- **Escrow services**—For big ticket items where the consequences of fraud are very severe, the buyer and seller may employ a third party to help manage the transaction. Companies such as i-Escrow and TradeSafe provide escrow services. The buyer sends payment to the escrow agent who informs the seller that payment has been received. The seller then ships the item. If the buyer does not complain to the escrow agent about delivery or condition of the goods within a specified period of time, then the escrow agent releases payment to the seller. The escrow agent takes a percentage of the sale for this service—about 5%.

- **Valuation services**—Valuation services help the buyer get an independent appraisal of the value of the seller's goods. The appraiser takes a percentage of the sale to offer this service.

- **Discussion groups**—Auction houses become communities in their own right with discussion groups in which the players can interact. Discussion groups are available for many item categories such as collectibles.

Exhibit 7 - 1   eBay Home Page

Source: www.ebay.com. These materials have been reproduced by Prentice Hall with the permission of eBay Inc. Copyright © eBay Inc. All rights reserved.

How do Auction Houses Make Money?

Some auction houses such as Yahoo! charge no fees and make their money by selling ads. Others such as eBay are fee supported. Auction house fees generally fall into the following categories:

- **Listing fees**—Listing fees are paid by the seller in order to list her item for auction. Generally this is a nominal fee of at most a few dollars.

- **Featuring fees**—Featuring fees are paid by the seller in order to make her item stand out in the listings. The item might appear on the home page or at the top of the listings for a particular category or in boldfaced type, and so forth. Featuring fees can be pricey.

- **Sales fees**—The seller pays sales fees to the auction house at the end of a successful auction. The house receives a percentage of the high bid—around 2.5%.

Armed with this brief overview, this exercise will send you to eBay in order to view an auction. You'll need to register at eBay, but don't worry - registration is free. Start by visiting eBay at www.ebay.com. A screen similar to Exhibit 7 - 1 will greet you.

1. First let's start with statistics
   a. How many items are on sale right now?
   b. How many categories does eBay provide to list items?
   c. How do you think eBay chooses its categories for organizing sale items?
   d. Do you think that having so many categories might cause sellers to list under the wrong category?

2. Go ahead and register—"It's free!" Were you required to provide credit card information as part of the registration process? Why or why not?

3. What steps are required in order to sell an item?

4. What steps are required in order to buy an item?

5. Find the link to "Big Ticket Items." (Hint: The link may be located on the site map page). Choose an item for which the auction has already been completed.
   a. Complete the following table:

Item	Number of Bids	Number of Bidders	High Bid

b.   Does the number of bids match the number of bidders? If not, then why not?

c.   Investigate the reputations of the seller and high bidder for the item by reviewing comments made about them by other eBayers. Complete the following chart:

Seller

	Past 7 days	Past month	Past 6 months
Positive			
Neutral			
Negative			
Total			

Buyer

	Past 7 days	Past month	Past 6 months
Positive			
Neutral			
Negative			
Total			

d.   Quote what you feel to be a representative comment made about the seller:

e.   Quote what you feel to be a representative comment made about the buyer.

f.   Based on your investigation, do you think that the transaction will be successful? Why or why not?

Online Retailing: "e-tailing"

Online retailing grows exponentially each year. Most products and services can now be purchased online. These include CDs, books, automobiles, insurance, furniture, and even home mortgages. Some of the larger online retailers such as Amazon and CDNow are established brands. Online retailing involves a number of distribution functions which may be performed either by the retailer or are outsourced to a third party such as Digital River. The functions include Web store design and hosting, order processing, order fulfillment, credit authorization, inventory management, merchandising, data warehousing and mining, and customer service.

- **Web store design**—Design describes the actual creation of the store and layout of the pages. The best designs are intuitive and easy to navigate.

- **Web store hosting**—Hosting means making the site publicly accessible by providing a computer system and Internet connection. The keys to Web hosting are keeping the store open and minimizing customer wait. The store is kept open by having redundant computer systems located in different parts of the country. If one site goes down the system transparently transfers all traffic to the others. Customer wait is minimized by maintaining high speed connections to the Internet, maintaining multiple high speed servers (server farms), and by using efficient software.

- **Order processing**—Order processing should be user friendly and safe. The best systems provide customers with good feedback throughout the order process. The order processing system manages an electronic shopping cart for the customer, provides the customer with a secure form to fill out, runs a credit authorization and notifies the warehouse to ship the item.

- **Order fulfillment**—Order fulfillment includes shipping and handling of the order. Web retailers often ship from warehouses strategically located near airports served by package delivery companies such as UPS and FedEx.

- **Merchandising**—Merchandising includes increasing site traffic, cross selling, and bundling products. Improving site construction so that the site will appear higher in the search engine rankings can increase site traffic. Cross selling includes suggesting compatible products to customers—in fast food terms, "Would you like fries with that?"

- **Relationship marketing**—Relationship marketing has become especially important on the Internet as software allows retailers to track their customers' identities and preferences. This software allows customers to be greeted by name and allows retailers to make product suggestions in keeping with customers' tastes. The software that assists in predicting customer preferences is called collaborative filtering software. It works by finding other customers who share your preferences and then suggesting products to you which interested those other customers.

- **Data Warehousing and data mining**—Online retailers collect a tremendous amount of data about their customers and sales. Analysis of these data helps them redesign their Web sites to feature high demand products, as well as assisting in product mix and pricing decisions.

- **Customer service**—There is a new generation of highly sophisticated software which assists e-tailers with customer service. One of the premier products in this category is called eGain. The eGain software scans incoming e-mail and then automatically routes it to the appropriate customer representative. The software also composes a suggested response to the message which the customer representative may accept or modify.

While e-tailers can perform all of the above functions themselves, some choose to hire other firms to provide these services—this is called outsourcing. Outsourcing distribution channel functions is a growing trend on the Internet. Since virtually all functions can be outsourced, the Internet allows for the creation of a virtual online business—one that runs no computer systems, employs no information systems staff, manages no inventory and fulfills no orders. Some companies such as Digital River and Pandesic provide comprehensive outsourcing of almost the entire business while others will outsource individual functions. You can even have a separate outsourcers manage each of the retail functions.

In this exercise you are going to build your own online store. Yahoo! Store is a comprehensive solution for small businesses seeking to establish an online storefront. Visit Yahoo! Store at store.yahoo.com.

6. Go ahead and test drive the store. You will actually create an online store in minutes. This is a free store with a catch—it expires after 10 days unless you pay the registration fee. You can sell anything you want at your store—don't worry, no one can place a real order. Looking for ideas? How about some stuff you have lying around your room? Once you have created the store make a printout of the home page and give it to your professor along with the URL for the store. The URL will be of the form store.yahoo.com/yourname.

7. Now complete the following chart listing the retail functions provided by Yahoo! store. Hint: you may need to explore some of the other items on the Yahoo! Store home page to answer these questions.

Function	Provided by Yahoo! Store (Y/N)?
Web store design	
Web store hosting	
Order processing	
Electronic shopping cart	
Secure order form	
Credit authorization	
Warehouse notification	
Order fulfillment	
Merchandising	
Relationship marketing	
Data Warehousing and data mining	
Customer Service	

8. What type of retail operation defines your store (e.g., department store)? Explain in terms of amount of service and product assortment.

9. Who is your target market and what market position will your store occupy?

10. What is the cost of running a store on Yahoo! Store?

11. Who are some of Yahoo! Store's more prominent clients?

12. What steps would you take to advertise your store?

Leveraging Technology

Site Rating Services

As sites proliferate it will become increasingly difficult for consumers to distinguish between reputable and non-reputable sites. Consumers will increasingly need to rely on reference services to select retail products and services. One rating service, Bizrate, is particularly interesting. Many Web sites agree to let Bizrate randomly sample their customer bases. They are like the J. D. Powers of the Web. The customers are surveyed immediately after completing the purchase and then again after the product is delivered ("exit survey"). The cumulative responses along different dimensions are then published on the Bizrate site. The dimensions include:

Pre-purchase	Post-purchase
▪ Price	▪ On-time Delivery
▪ Product	▪ Product
▪ Selection	▪ Availability
▪ Product	▪ (In-Stock)
▪ Information	▪ Customer Support
▪ Web site	▪ Ease of Returns
▪ Aesthetics	▪ Customer Loyalty
▪ Web site	
▪ Navigation	

Additionally Bizrate indicates the availability of the following services on each site.

- ▪ Secure ordering/payment system (SSL/SET)
- ▪ Online ordering shopping chart system
- ▪ Online order tracking system
- ▪ Customer information privacy
- ▪ Gift wrapping
- ▪ Live customer support
- ▪ International shipping
- ▪ Product search

While Bizrate accepts no advertising or sponsorship, it makes money by selling detailed copies of reports to the merchants. These include trends over time along each dimension.

---

[1] Sawhney, Mohanbir (1999), "Making New Markets," *Business 2.0* (May).

Chapter **8**

The Net as Marketing Communication Medium

Estimated time: 80 minutes

Learning Objectives

- Understand Web sites as electronic brochures

- Explain two important types of online advertising

- Describe how Web sites can be used for direct marketing

- Discuss the use of Web sites for PR with various stakeholders

- Discover places to send electronic press releases announcing new Web sites

- Tell how the Web can be used for sales promotions

Online Marketing Communication

The Net is an important tool for marketing communication messages between marketers and their desired audiences. This, along with marketing research and distribution functions, is a major strength and use of the Net for marketers. Organizations promote to various audiences through advertising, public relations, sales promotion, personal selling, and direct marketing. Currently, marketers use all marketing communication tools online except for personal selling. In this chapter we discuss ways that firms use the Internet to promote their products, and then we give you a chance to explore the Web site of a firm that has done an excellent job of online promotion.

Advertising

For marketers, the Net is similar to a magazine or a television. These media have content (i.e., articles and programs) and they sell advertising. Some content providers offer classified advertising to Net users. Other content providers, who are especially successful at drawing large audiences, sell designated advertising space on their Web pages. These ads are called banners and buttons. You have already visited many Web sites and seen ads on their pages. Two sophisticated advertising techniques are keyword ads and ad servers.

- **Keyword ads**— This technique is used by some of the search engines to target banner ads to the search terms that a user enters. For example, if you type Toyota as a search term, you might see ads for car dealerships or automobile parts at Toyota or its competitors.

- **Ad servers**— Third party firms such as DoubleClick sell advertising and then deliver it to target users along with requested Web pages. Sophisticated ad servers actually track the pages that users visit around the Web to learn their psychographic profiles—"you are what you view". They then target ads based on the profile. Suppose you went from a site about music to check out the news at MSNBC. DoubleClick might deliver an ad for CD's along with the MSNBC page because they know you are a music lover. This is a brilliant strategy for advertisers because they know their ads are being delivered to appropriate users.

Sponsorships are another type of Web advertising. On television, the Hallmark Hall of Fame is an example of a program (content) sponsorship. On the Web, a company such as Kraft, develops recipe content and pays to place it on a Web site targeted to homemakers. The only way a user can tell that Kraft paid for the sponsorship is to look for logos or mentions of Kraft brands on the page. This type of advertising is not very common in traditional media, but generates about half of all Web advertising dollars.

Public Relations

The Web is an important vehicle for public relations activities. PR creates goodwill among an organization's stakeholders. It is important for a company to communicate with customers, employees, the government, the media, shareholders, and many other groups in order to influence public opinion. PR communication tools include special events, publicity through press releases, public service campaigns, and publications such as newsletters, brochures and annual reports. The term "brochureware" emerged to define Web sites that contain only product or company information. On the Web, companies use PR in some of the following ways:

- Customer service communication with consumers via e-mail or Web forms
- Online special events, such as the Victoria Secret Fashion Show in early 1999
- Community building through chat rooms and discussion groups
- Online information for various publics, such as product information and annual reports
- Electronic press releases for PR publicity

Sales Promotions

Sales promotions are short-term incentives that aid the movement of product from producer to consumer. Some sales promotion tactics directed at consumers include coupons, rebates, samples, premiums, contests and sweepstakes. Most of these are currently offered on the Web, however, coupons, samples and contests/sweepstakes are the most widely used.

- **Coupons**—Some firms, such as J. Crew deliver coupons in e-mail responses to dissatisfied customers. Others, such as Coupon Pages (www.couponpages.com) and Hot Coupons (www.hotcoupons.com) provide electronic coupons on the Web. Consumers print them or have them sent to their homes.

- **Samples**—Many software firms allow users to download free 30-day trials of a particular program. Sampling encourages users to purchase the product after they've found it indispensable. CDNow and other music retailers allow users to sample a small portion of a sound track prior to purchase.

- **Contests/Sweepstakes**—The Web is full of free giveaways. Users can enter contests by submitting answers to questions or writing why they like a particular product in 25 words or less. You can enter sweepstakes and win a wide assortment of cool prizes if your name is drawn. The exercise in this chapter gives you a chance to enter a sweepstake of your choice.

Personal Selling

The Net is not used for personal selling because the computer mediates communication between audience and content provider: it is *impersonal*. However, the Net is used to generate leads for salespeople. For example, Herman Miller, producer of office furniture, sells most of its products to businesses. A visit to their Web site at www.hermanmiller.com offers both business and government users a chance to contact a salesperson directly.

Direct Marketing

Direct marketing is communication to individually targeted users for the purpose of generating an immediate response—it is sometimes called 1:1 marketing. As a strategy, direct marketing is a bit confusing because it can appear in the form of advertising, sales promotion, or any other promotion mix element. For example, a coupon generated at the grocery store based on your particular purchase and a telemarketing phone call are both considered direct marketing. Marketers increasingly include direct marketing as a fifth promotion mix strategy because of its growing importance and its unique differences from the other communication mix tools. Traditional direct marketing strategies include direct mail (catalogs are a huge part of this), FAX messages, telemarketing, and direct response advertising such as infomercials and other selectively targeted ads with response mechanisms such as a 1-800 telephone number.

The Internet provides outstanding direct marketing opportunities for marketers because it allows for immediate two-way communication between customers/prospects and firms. It is especially important in the business-to-business market. Some online direct marketing tactics are the following:

- **Outgoing e-mail**—Many firms build e-mail databases of customers and prospective customers and use them to send occasional messages. 3Com regularly sends e-mail notes to PalmPilot users suggesting product usage tips and recommending hardware or software updates based on the user's specific PalmPilot version. Any e-mail you receive from a firm that includes a hyperlink to a Web site is direct marketing. All e-mail messages that firms tailor to selected individuals and that request a response are direct marketing: the response can be anything from a reply to a purchase.

- **Personalized Web pages**—After registering at a Web site, users may be greeted personally on their next visit and asked to respond with a purchase. An example of this occurs at Amazon.com when you log on. The Amazon home page greets you by name, and presents personal book or music suggestions tailored to your reading/listening habits, giving you a way to order them immediately.

- **Ad servers**—We described these in the previous section on advertising. When an ad server sends an individualized ad to a particular user this is also considered direct marketing because the user can click on the ad to visit the advertised site.

Direct marketing is a particularly powerful tool because it helps firms to build relationships with their customers. Direct, personalized communication assists firms in retaining and building customer business over the long run: a much more efficient tactic than continually finding new customers. The Internet, and e-mail in particular, are "killer apps" for direct marketing relationship-building.

Marketing Communication at McDonald's

McDonald's sells hamburgers. Of course, you already knew that. Their success has had something to do with their menu items but a lot more to do with their savvy marketing promotions. In this exercise we look at their online promotional techniques, evaluating McDonald's PR techniques, and discovering online advertising opportunities for them. Visit www.mcdonalds.com.

Public Relations

1. McDonald's web site is a good example of how sites can be used for public relations. First, the site itself is a PR tool, similar to a product brochure that lists and describes its products—everything from food to merchandise. Second, it discusses many community services, including the Ronald McDonald Houses. Next, it helps customers find the nearest restaurant. Understanding that most of us know where our local McDonald's is, these savvy marketers introduced a trip planner that shows you where to find restaurants along the way. Finally, the McDonald's site communicates with many stakeholder

groups in addition to consumers. Cruise the site and find at least three other stakeholders who are targeted on the site and complete the following table by describing the types of information McDonald's provides to each group.

Stakeholder	Type of Information

2. McDonald's sponsors many sport teams, a beneficial PR activity. Locate and describe one sporting event described at the site.

Press Releases

3. What should McDonald's do to publicize its Web site? One easy way to advertise the address for a Web site is to put it on all promotional materials at the restaurant and in all ads. Another way is to ask related sites to provide free links to its page. Name one Web site that might want to link to McDonald's as a service to its audience, and explain why you think it is appropriate. (Hint: remember you can actually find out who is linked to McDonald's using the link operator you learned about in Chapter 1.)

4. A final PR step involves sending press releases to the search engines, and many other directories known for free Web site listing. For a summary of how to publicize a Web site, visit www.submit-it.com. After reviewing their free information on how to publicize a site (a "Web site marketing primer" is currently in the *services* section), list and briefly describe seven major ways one could publicize the McDonald's Web site. Note: if this section is not available when you do this exercise, search for other sites that discuss Web site promotion.

Method	Description
1.	
2.	
3.	
4.	
5.	

Method	Description
6.	
7.	

Note that Submit-it will do all the work of publicizing your site if you are willing to pay them. Some of the services like Submit-it claim to be able to have your site listed in the first screen that appears when a Web user queries for a related term using a search engine.

Advertising

5. McDonald's may even *pay* others to provide a link to its home page. These links are either in the form of banner ads or hyperlinks within content which the user can click-through to visit the advertised site. To explore sponsorship options for McDonald's, visit www.homearts.com, a site that provides lots of information and ideas for women about family and home. The folks at McDonald's enjoy a similar target market and family image, so this is a potential advertising sponsorship opportunity (at a mere $50/month to reach 1000 users). Examine *cool tools* and *partners* pages and come up with an idea for McDonalds. What topic could McDonalds write about, and what content could it provide that would help advertise products and naturally provide a link to their site? An interactive tool based on McDonald's products would be especially strong.

Topic	Basic content/tool idea

6. Help McDonald's figure out where to buy banner ads on the Web. Suggest three sites that might be good ideas and tell why you picked each one. Hint: the information from question 3 might help.

Site	Reason

Exhibit 8 - 1 Freestuff2000.com
Source: www.freestuff2000.com

Sales Promotions Galore

7. Contests, sweepstakes and games are popping up all over the Web. They build excitement about brands, and can encourage purchase. More specific to the Web, they draw the audience to a site and keep them returning. Sweepstakes are pure luck of the draw. Sponsors cannot require a purchase because then the sales promotion is considered a lottery and would be covered under gambling law. Conversely, contests require skill, such as correctly answering a trivia question. Visit the games and giveaways page at www.freestuff2000.com/giveaways, and you'll see a screen like that in Exhibit 8 - 1. In their sweepstakes section find a prize that is appealing to you. Follow the link to the site sponsoring the sweepstakes. What is the Web address and company name for the site sponsoring this sweepstakes?

8. What is the first prize (the one that drew *you* to this page)?

9. What marketing purpose do you think this organization has for running the sweepstakes?

Putting It All Together

10. Now that you've seen a few ways firms communicate with consumers using the Internet and learned a lot about the Net from this book, make a summary table demonstrating what you've learned. For each marketing communication tool, tell whether you think the Internet or traditional media (e.g., print, broadcast, postal mail) is better and why.

Tool	I = Internet T = traditional	Why?
Advertising		
Public Relations		
Sales Promotion		
Personal Selling		
Direct Marketing		

Leveraging Technology

Rotating and Targeted Ad Banners

Hit your browser's refresh or reload button on Yahoo!'s web site and you are likely to find that the banner ad on the page changes. Yahoo! Sells its inventory of banner slots on a rotating basis. Advertisers are guaranteed a certain number of impressions over a period of time but other ads will be interspersed with theirs. This is not unlike the ads that rotate on a scoreboard during professional sporting events. However, sporting events have a distinct advantage—they know the characteristics of their audience and therefore can target ads to their needs. Magazines and newspapers have a similar feature called "selective binding." Advertisers in Time Magazine, for example, can select from among over 200 different versions: any market from doctors, business executives, or students to very specific geographic areas. It is likely that the issue of Time that you receive as a student will contain different ads and even a few different articles than issues created for other markets. In order to achieve the same level of efficiency in the online world, the industry developed targeted ads. The ad changes or rotates based upon the search words that you type into the search engine. Targeted ads cost more per impression because advertisers are more effectively able to reach their target based on psychographics (interests of users).

Even more impressive are ad networks such as DoubleClick which are able to track and target users as they move from site to site! How does DoubleClick track users across sites? It stores a file called a cookie on the user's computer that identifies the user by number. Whenever the user visits a site in the DoubleClick network, DoubleClick reads the cookie, looks up and/or modifies the user's profile, and then targets an appropriate ad. See Exhibit 8 - 2. The process is very efficient from a direct marketing point and extremely successful. DoubleClick delivers over 1.5 billion ads EACH DAY! Nonetheless, targeted ads do raise legal and ethical issues concerning privacy— especially since most users do not know they are being tracked. Is DoubleClick tracking you? Find the cookie files on your hard drive to see. Internet Explorer stores each cookie in a separate file in the Cookies directory. Netscape Navigator, by contrast, places all of the cookies in the same file called cookies.txt. Use the Windows find files feature to search for *cookie*. This will find cookies.txt (for Netscape) as well as the Cookies directory (for Internet Explorer). You can open cookie files in a text editor by double clicking on them. Exhibit 8 - 3 shows the contents of a cookie file for a newly installed computer. The user has visited exactly one site, www.travelocity.com. However, since Travelocity uses DoubleClick as their ad server a DoubleClick cookie is also written to the user's computer.

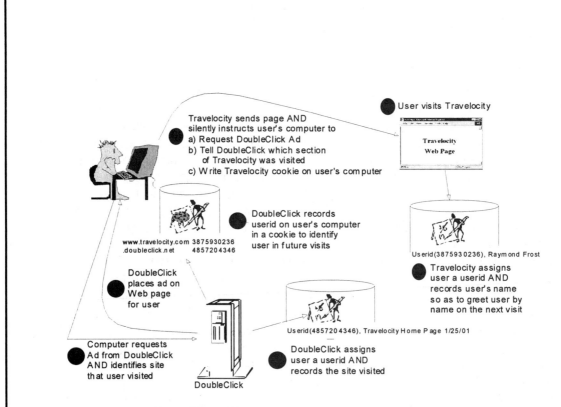

Exhibit 8 - 2 Tracking Users Site to Site

Netscape HTTP Cookie File
http://www.netscape.com/newsref/std/cookie_spec.html
This is a generated file! Do not edit.

www.travelocity.com	FALSE	/	FALSE	3875930236	grtng	1
.doubleclick.net	TRUE	/	FALSE	4857204346	id	A

Exhibit 8 - 3 Netscape Cookie File (cookie.txt)

At this point the user has two cookies on her computer—one from Travelocity and one from DoubleClick. The Travelocity cookie will allow Travelocity to greet the user by name on a subsequent visit. The DoubleClick cookie will be used to track the user around the Internet. The next time that the user visits a site on the DoubleClick network, DoubleClick will be able to target an ad to that user for a travel related service.

Glossary

Ad server—Third party firms sell advertising, store it on a server, and deliver it to target users along with requested Web pages.

Bandwidth—The data transfer capacity of a network system—how much information can be sent from one place to another in a given period of time. There are many ways to measure this—for example, the number of megabytes transferred per second.

Banner ad—A rectangular space appearing on a Web site, paid for by an advertiser, which allows the user to click-through to the advertiser's Web site.

Browser—A browser is a software program that runs on a personal computer and provides a graphical user interface (GUI) to the Web. The two most popular browsers are Netscape Navigator and Microsoft Internet Explorer.

Brochureware—A site that provides information about the company's products and services. Brochureware provides an excellent opportunity to brand as well as to develop a relationship with the consumer and other stakeholders.

Caching—Phenomenon that occurs when access providers or browsers store or buffer Web page data in a temporary location on their networks or in their disk space to speed access and reduce traffic. Reduces the number of measured page views at the original content site.

Cookie A persistent piece of information, stored on the user's local hard drive, that is keyed to a specific server (and even a file pathway or directory location at the server) and is passed back to the server as part of the transaction that takes place when the user's browser again crosses the specific server/path combination.

Demographics—Demographics are vital statistics about people such as their age, income and ethnicity.

Digital products—Text, audio, and video that are converted to digital form for online distribution.

Directory search—A search that requires the user navigate by progressively more specific subjects until they find the information for which they are looking.

Disintermediation—The process of eliminating traditional intermediaries. Eliminating intermediaries has the potential to reduce costs since each intermediary adds to the price of the product.

Domain name—Domain names are used to address sites on the Internet. The top-level domain names are com, edu, gov, net, and org. Second level domain names usually correspond to familiar trademarks like Coca-Cola, McDonalds, Pepsi, etc.

Electronic business (e-business) Includes all electronic and Internet activities conducted by organizations such as e-mail, e-commerce, stakeholder communication, and database activities. This term and e-commerce are often used interchangeably.

Electronic commerce (e-commerce) Includes buying/selling online, digital value creation, virtual marketplaces and storefronts, and new distribution channel intermediaries.[1]

Electronic marketing (e-marketing) Includes all electronic data and applications used for the marketing of a firm's products, such as customer profile and marketing mix information, and their strategic use to increase sales or reduce marketing costs.

Environmental scan—In an environmental scan, the organization collects and interprets information about the trends, events and relationships which might affect its marketing effort.

Ethernet—Ethernet refers to the most popular transport technology standard used in local area networks (LANs).

Home page—A Home Page is first page that you see when you visit a site (e.g., www.honda.com). Sites often have many different home pages if they host many different users. In this case you must know the subdirectory where the users home page is located (e.g., faculty.cob.ohiou.edu/frostr).

HTML (hypertext markup language)—A simple coding system used to format documents for viewing by Web clients. Web pages are written in this standard specification.

Hyperlink—Hyperlinks are text or graphics that link to other pages on the Web.

Internet—The Internet is the global inter-network of computers. Major uses of the Internet include e-mail and Web browsing.

Intranet—Intranets employ Internet technology to form home pages that are internal to a company. The Intranet serves as an easily accessible repository for corporate information—anything from strategic targets to health plans. Intranets capitalize on the fact that most organizations distribute far more information internally than they do to the outside world. Intranets are also called corporate portals.

ISP (Internet Service Provider)—Company that has a network of servers (mail, news, Web, and the like), routers, and modems attached to a permanent, high-speed Internet "backbone" connection. Subscribers can then dial into the local network to gain Internet access.

Keyword search—Open text searches are also called keyword searches. These searches scan the Web looking for a word or group of words that were entered as a search string. The search engine then lists links to pages that it determines are most relevant to the search string. A page with more matches is considered more likely to be relevant.

Link—See hyperlink

Modem—A modem is a device that translates computer signals into sound waves and back again to allow two computers to communicate over a phone line. Its name comes from the fact that it modulates computer signals to sound and demodulates sound back to computer signals. Today's fastest modems receive data at about 50,000 characters per second.

Net—Net is short for Internet.

Page—An HTML (hypertext markup language) document that may contain text, images, and other online elements, such as Java applets and multimedia files.

Primary data—Primary data are information gathered for the purpose of researching a particular problem.

Random sample—A random sample is the key to marketing research. When subjects are chosen at random then every member of the population has an equal chance of being chosen. Random samples help guarantee that the results of the sample will generalize accurately to the population.

Secondary data—Secondary data are information that has already been collected for another purpose but helps with the current problem.

Shopping agents—Programs that allow the consumer to rapidly compare prices and features within product categories. Shopping agents implicitly negotiate prices downward on behalf of the consumer by listing companies in order of best price first.

Site—A site is a home page on the Internet.

Sponsorship—A type of advertising where a company creates content and pays to place it on someone else's Web site.

Syndicated sales—Web sites paying a commission on referrals. Syndicated selling rewards the referring Web site by paying a 7% to 15% commission on the sale. Paying the commission, like all channel intermediary costs, has the effect of inflating the price of the item or lowering company profits.

URL—The unique address of a Web site: for example, www.unr.edu

Usenet—Worldwide network of thousands of computer systems with a decentralized administration. The Usenet systems exist to transmit postings to special-interest newsgroups.

Web—The World Wide Web (WWW) defines a standard for navigating between computers on the Internet using hyperlinks.

Web site—The virtual location for an organization's presence on the Worldwide Web, usually made up of several Web pages and a single home page designated by a unique URL.